W9-BZW-003

AROUND THE
WORLD IN 60 SECONDS

AROUND THE WORLD IN 60 SECONDS

THE NAS DAILY JOURNEY

1,000 DAYS. 64 COUNTRIES. 1 BEAUTIFUL PLANET.

NUSEIR YASSIN

WITH BRUCE KLUGER

HarperOne
An Imprint of HarperCollins*Publishers*

HarperOne

AROUND THE WORLD IN 60 SECONDS. Copyright © 2019 by Nuseir Yassin. All rights reserved. Printed in the United States of America. No part of this book may be used or reproduced in any manner whatsoever without written permission except in the case of brief quotations embodied in critical articles and reviews. For information, address HarperCollins Publishers, 195 Broadway, New York, NY 10007.

HarperCollins books may be purchased for educational, business, or sales promotional use. For information, please email the Special Markets Department at SPsales@harpercollins.com.

FIRST EDITION

Designed by Kris Tobiassen of Matchbook Digital

All photos courtesy of the author except page 170 by Kevin Carter / Sygma / Sygma via Getty; and pages ii (all except top center), vi, x, 16, 32, 38, 58, 82, 142, 198, 226 by iStock.

Library of Congress Cataloging-in-Publication Data is available upon request.

ISBN 978-0-06-293267-9

19 20 21 22 23 LSC 10 9 8 7 6 5 4 3 2

FOR THE 11,829,656 PEOPLE
WHO BELIEVED IN ME.

"Let's suppose you were able, every night, to dream any dream you wanted to dream. Naturally, as you began on this adventure of dreams, you would fulfill all of your wishes. You would have every kind of pleasure during your sleep. And after several nights you would say, 'Well, that was pretty great, but now let's have a surprise. Let's have a dream that isn't under control, where something is going to happen to me and I don't know what that something will be.' Then you would get more and more adventurous and you would make further and further gambles on what you would dream. And finally, you would dream where you are now."

—ALAN WATTS, "THE DREAM OF LIFE"

CONTENTS

EASTER ISLAND, CHILE

INTRODUCTION

Okay, I'll admit it—I momentarily lost my mind.

The date was October 2, 2016, and I was on Day 176 of my worldwide adventure. By then, Nas Daily had visited some twenty countries and sixty-three cities, and I'd just come off a two-day trip to Chile—one day in Santiago, where I'd grabbed some awesome footage from the roof of Gran Torre, the tallest skyscraper in Latin America; and the next day in the port city of Valparaiso, where I'd shot the town's famous candy-colored cottages and enjoyed a sunset dinner by the bay with some new friends.

But this day—day three in Chile—was the reason I'd made the trip there.

"I'm heading to the most remote island in the world," I had told my Facebook followers a few days earlier, slapping a map onto the table like an overeager schoolkid delivering a geography report. "Here! Right here! This island—Easter Island! It's going to take forever to get to, but I think it's going to be worth it."

And so there I was that following Sunday, standing on the shore of sixty-three square miles of impossible beauty floating on the easternmost point of the Polynesian Triangle, and, basically, flipping out. I'd been told that Easter

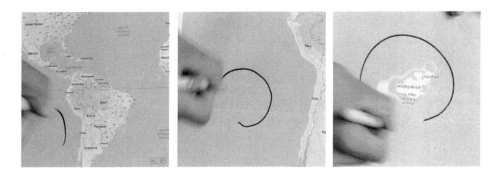

Island was an awesome place to visit—that's why I was there. But no travel brochure on the planet can prepare you for its unexpected assault on your senses, when the wind and the surf and the overwhelmingly beautiful nature knock you off-balance, and you suddenly feel as if everything in your life has pointed you to this space and this place and this precise moment in time—and nothing else matters.

"Oh, my God! This is a sick shot!" I yelled into the lens of my Canon digital over the opening image, the wind rippling my T-shirt and my smile clearly combustible. "I made it to Easter Island! This place is ridiculously insane!"

What followed was two and a half days of unchecked euphoria as I criss-crossed the island with abandon, my breathless commentary punctuated by one stunning shot after another:

Angry waves slamming against the deep-red cliffs on the northern coastline.

Time-lapse footage of fat clouds tearing over a mountain ridge.

Wild horses lazily grazing a field of tall golden grass.

And panoramic sweeps of the countless hills that dot the island, each one carpeted in soft, green vegetation.

And, of course, there were the moai, Easter Island's huge, iconic sculptures of human heads carved by the Rapa Nui people nearly eight centuries ago. Standing guard on the island's perimeter, facing inward to protect its inhabitants, these monolithic behemoths—887 of them altogether, the largest of them rising 71 feet and weighing 150 tons—are at once breathtaking and humbling, and I wasn't going to let my time with them go wasted.

"This is fucking beautiful!" I told the camera, pointing to a lone moai on a hillside. "It's a face! In the middle of the island! There's nothing here, nothing around. The nearest piece of land is six hours away from here!"

I rented a bright-red Kawasaki Brute Force ATV, climbed on, and tore across the island, leaving behind any last shred of emotional inhibition I had carried with me since embarking on this journey. With each new destination, I became a little more wild, a little more free—taking ballet leaps across the screen, sprinting through a grove of coconut trees, and lying down in the grass, whispering my innermost thoughts into the camera.

"I can't get enough of this nature," I said. "It's just so *beautiful!*"

Now comfortable with the island's topography—and blessed with un-usually perfect weather—I launched my drone six hundred feet into the skies above Easter Island and let her do her thing. As always, she crushed it, as she

EASTER ISLAND, CHILE

swept over the enchanted landscape and returned a dizzying array of pictures that only God deserves to see.

"You wanna see heaven? Look right there!" I said to my invisible viewer after my brave little quadcopter sent back an arresting collection of aerials above Anakena Beach.

When I put the clips together for that night's Facebook post, the background music I selected was the theme song from the movie *Gravity*—a fitting choice, I figured, given that every moment I spent on Easter Island made me feel weightless.

Three days passed in a blink, and on my final morning, I packed up my gear and prepared to leave—and not a moment too soon, it turned out. Evidently, my over-the-top enthusiasm for this wild Chilean outpost (and my, um, slightly illegal droning activities) had attracted attention. The bad kind.

"Ka ui riva tiva te kapi ne," the park rangers wrote on my exit ticket—which, roughly translated from Rapa Nui, means, "You're not welcome anymore."

That's okay. Chilly dismissal notwithstanding, I had experienced something magical during my seventy-two hours on Easter Island—something I would feel again and again as Nas Daily's originally planned 60-day world tour turned into 260 days. Then a year. Then two years. Then more.

It was the same feeling of heart-stopping awe that I experienced on nearly every leg of this grand journey since 2016:

Watching Mount Fuji break through the clouds on a foggy morning on Honshu Island in Japan.

Standing in the shadow of Zuma Rock in Nigeria and scanning its twenty-four-hundred-foot face for the ghosts that legendarily live there.

Stepping into a six-hundred-year-old cathedral in Cologne, Germany, or a woodland sanctuary in Rishikesh, India, or a Buddhist temple in Phuket, Thailand.

Sleeping beneath the stars in the Sahara Desert in Morocco, or taking a mud bath in the Dead Sea.

Walking the ancient streets of Jerusalem and Palestine.

And throughout it all, no matter the country, I continued to witness up-close the indestructibility of the human spirit and the overwhelming power of the human heart. In Arabic, *Nas* means "people," and on this wild adventure, it was the people I cared about most.

Like the eleven-year-old schoolgirl I met in Myanmar who taught herself seven languages so she could work as a tour guide to support her family of eight.

Or the young man in India, a Nas Daily follower, who saw online that I was in his country and feeling ill, so he tracked me down and brought me to his home so that his family could care for me.

Or the Syrian widow living in a refugee camp in Greece whose family had been broken and scattered by the ravages of war. When she told me her story, she spoke without any trace of bitterness or anger and then explained how she spends her days, gathering what meager food rations she receives and cooking meals for the dozens of children who live in her camp. "It is my honor to do this," she said.

This is why I quit my job.

This is why I travel the world.

This is why I started Nas Daily.

On April 10, 2016, I bought a one-way ticket to Nairobi, Kenya, and set out on an odyssey whose end I did not know. The plan was relatively simple: cover as much ground as I could in sixty days and chronicle my travels on Facebook, filming one video each day.

Granted, the idea was stupid, but it wasn't like I was unfamiliar with the rigors of travel—waking up in a new country, negotiating the culture shock, finding my way around. Indeed, I'd traveled a fair amount in my twenty-four years, and not just to safe vacation destinations. I'd been to Moscow and

Cambodia, Sri Lanka and North Korea—and I grew up in the Middle East, where the feeling of war never stops.

I was no stranger, either, to recording my exploits on camera. Two years earlier, I'd made a stunt video, traveling to eleven countries over three months with the singular mission of solving a Rubik's Cube. In each new city, I would hand the Cube to anyone I saw—locals, tourists, even animals—and ask them to give it one turn and one turn only. It was a crazy idea that ultimately paid off: ninety days, eighty-four people, and one Thai monkey later, the Cube was solved.

But this trip, I knew, was going to be different, mostly because I wasn't really sure why I was taking it or what I hoped to achieve. Its very open-endedness—its unscripted, unchartered unpredictability—was *the whole purpose*.

What I did know, however, was that before I set off on my trip, my life was becoming routine. And if there's anything I hate, it's routine. My LinkedIn profile painted a portrait of a smart, enterprising young man who kept his head down and did his job. But that's not what I saw when I looked in the

THE RUBIK'S CUBE CHALLENGE

mirror. What I saw was a hairy, twenty-four-year-old Palestinian-Israeli kid with an Ivy League education who was ready to walk away from a sweet, high-paying job for the adventure of a lifetime.

But I'm getting ahead of myself. Let me back up.

I was born and raised in the tiny village of Arraba, Israel, a tight cluster of white stone dwellings tucked within the slopes of the Sakhnin Valley in the Lower Galilee. Not exactly a bustling front-page destination on Travelocity, Arraba boasts twenty-five thousand residents, zero tourists, and about half a million potholes. The city is surrounded by ample farmland—olives, watermelons, onions—and its dominant structure is the Great Mosque, whose twelve-story minaret rises proudly above the neighboring Islamic architecture.

Arraba's greatest distinction, however, is its mere existence—an Arab city in a Jewish state—and even as a child I began to understand that you don't need a robust tourist trade or popular theme park to make your hometown special. What matters most are the people—that's the one thing you can't manufacture. And the people of Arraba are good people.

Especially in my household. I grew up in a warm and inviting home. We were neither poor nor rich—we were fine—and we took a genuine interest in each other's lives. Dad's a psychologist, mom's a schoolteacher, and I'm the second of four kids. We were never spoiled with material things or money (there wasn't much of it to go around), but we were spoiled with love and freedom.

ARRABA, ISRAEL

Looking back, I don't recall anything especially negative about my childhood, but I will say that I was a very shy kid—no social life at all. So I spent most of my days sitting in front of a computer and cruising the internet—learning, learning, learning. Say what you will about the web, there's nothing like Google to broaden the mind and skill set of a curious child.

The internet is where I learned to play the piano (though I still can't read sheet music).

It's where I learned to do finger tricks with a pencil (a social icebreaker that comes in handier than you might expect) and solve a Rubik's Cube in sixteen seconds (a personal record, by the way—I got lucky).

It's where I first discovered different lands and different cultures, long before I could afford an airline ticket to any of them.

And, most important, it's where I learned to speak English, mostly by watching American movies with Arab subtitles or hanging out in online gaming communities, where in addition to the basics, I learned a lot of useful swear words. Even offline, learning English became all-consuming for me. I'd practice while walking home from school, talking to myself. My personal goal was to speak without an accent and get all of my pronunciations correct. (I remember *salmon* being especially hard.)

By age nineteen, I had grown comfortable—too comfortable, in fact, and that was a problem. I didn't know it at the time—it would take me several years to figure it out—but for me, comfort is the first sign that things are not okay. There's a reason for the popularity of those dorm posters and T-shirts that bear the slogan "Life begins at the end of your comfort zone"—because it happens to be true. When you get comfortable, you stop growing, you stop producing, you plateau. And in 2011, that was my life.

Then something unexpected happened. A writer from Ohio named Martha (Marti) Moody flew to Israel to volunteer with the Arab-Israeli community. She was working with my high school English teacher, Jamal Assadi, so she came to my class to give us a lesson in writing. She'd brought her son Jack with her, and he and I forged a fast bond when I taught him my pencil-twirling trick (didn't I tell you it comes in handy?). We stayed in touch after he and his mom returned to Ohio.

A few months later, I got an email from Martha:

Hey, Little Big Nose—feel like coming to Ohio for a visit? Find your way over here and we'll put you up. We miss you.

I took Marti up on her offer, and while I was in Ohio, she suggested I visit her eldest son, Eli, who was a student at Harvard University.

This wasn't some random idea—Marti had plans for me. Apparently, she had spotted my restlessness and thought it would be a good idea to dangle the crazy idea of a Harvard education in front of me. Perhaps she saw academic potential. Or perhaps she just felt sorry for me, squandering my days back in Arraba, hanging out online and practicing my English swear words.

If that's the case, Marti wasn't all that wrong. Although my childhood was nothing less than loving, the culture of Arraba did not encourage a lot of moving around. Things like buying a new house or divorcing a spouse and relocating were rare in my village and the surrounding towns. People loved their land so much they'd rather die on it than leave it. So it was always a surprise when someone picked up and moved away—especially to the States.

That said, I bit at the Harvard bait—hard. From the moment I stepped onto that campus, I began seeing the world through crimson-colored glasses. This was going to be my next hill to climb, I decided, and it would take everything I had.

When I got back to Israel, I began researching Harvard's application process and did not like what I found: at the time, the school had a 3 percent admission rate, and if you were lucky enough to get accepted, the tuition was 60 grand a year. Nothing like hard numbers to suck the air out of a fantasy.

And yet the sheer absurdity of this dream—rural Arab boy becomes American Ivy Leaguer!—only made me lunge at it harder. Crazier things have happened. So I filled out the paperwork, submitted my high school transcript, applied for financial aid, and crossed my fingers.

Actually, I didn't even bother to cross my fingers—I knew I'd never get in.

And then . . . I got in.

I got in.

Holy shit. I'm going to Harvard.

As they say, with time comes wisdom, and in retrospect, I think my greatest takeaway from the four years I spent in the academic climes of Cambridge, Massachusetts, was the knowledge that we all possess the potential to take our lives up a notch—whether it's going to a better school, or buying a better home, or living a better life.

The common assumption about Harvard is that you need great grades and decent connections to get in, and all of that is true. But what you also need is a hunger—for anything. A hunger for photography. A hunger for math. A hunger for sports. A hunger for whatever it is that ignites that secret pilot light inside of you.

When I applied to Harvard, I wasn't just hungry, I was *starving*. And the funny thing is, I wasn't even entirely sure what I was starving for. So even before I graduated from Harvard, I began exploring different versions of myself to see whether any of them was, in fact, the *better me*. I knew that whatever talent I had dwelled in the world of tech; so between my sophomore and senior years, I spent my summers in New York City, teaming up with fellow dream-chasers in pursuit of that One Great Idea. We lived in a cheap walk-up in Harlem, worked in the cramped office space of a startup incubator, and dined out on sidewalk-vendor food-cart cuisine. If living outside of one's comfort zone truly is the secret to success, I should have been a mogul by age twenty.

But I wasn't—because mostly what I was doing for those two years was introducing myself to failure. Repeatedly.

In 2012, I built Kindify, an online platform for sharing, tracking, and rewarding individual acts of kindness across the social media world. Apparently, no good deed goes unpunished, because Kindify flopped.

HARVARD UNIVERSITY

Then I launched Branchly, a search engine that tied together all of your social media for better connectivity and networking. That tanked, too.

Then I came up with Downtime, a news aggregator that showed only stories that were one minute long. Nope.

Then I tried Oyster, a clothing rental company for travelers that I was certain would be a runaway hit. Buh-bye.

And finally I created Delphi, a music recommendation engine for restaurant background Muzak. You get the picture.

But here's the thing about failure: it's the default state of any startup; and the truth is, I still believe there's merit to all of the projects I tried to launch. I just wasn't the guy to make them. But more important, by the time I walked out of Harvard's gates as a new graduate in 2014, I'd already given myself a head start in the one course no college teaches—Real Life 101—and that gave me confidence.

And with confidence comes the ability to sell yourself.

And with the ability to sell yourself comes a job.

Which is why in September 2014, with the ink still wet on my Harvard diploma, I was hired full-time as a software engineer for the giant mobile payment service Venmo.

As an engineer, my job didn't involve the app itself. Instead, I was charged with handling the back infrastructure, dealing with the massive amounts of payment data Venmo collects—a figure that was often in the tens of billions of dollars—and sending it along to PayPal.

And I'm not going to lie—life at Venmo was pretty damn sweet. You go into the office (in Manhattan!), get a free, healthy breakfast, work at whatever kind of desk you want—sitting, standing—grab a free lunch, and work on an app that improves the lives of users around the world. And all of this while being surrounded by people you really like.

The pay didn't suck either: $120,000 a year.

So let's see: a good business, a great environment, fantastic pay? Yep, the perfect job.

Which is exactly why I had to quit.

"So let me get this straight," a friend said to me, "you're leaving Venmo because it's a *good job?*"

Admittedly, it sounded crazy. Here I was, fresh out of college, pulling down 120 Gs a year in a job that any sane person my age would die for. Common sense would dictate that I stick it out a little longer—I'd been there only twenty months—and see where it took me. In fact, given the success of the company and my own ambition, I probably could have dug in, risen in the ranks, and been a millionaire in ten years.

But it was that comfort-zone thing again.

And that hunger thing.

And a new thing I was feeling called anger.

I am quick to add that I wasn't angry at Venmo. As far as dream jobs go, it was pretty damn dreamy, and the people there couldn't have been nicer. What I was angry at was the whole idea that Venmo—or any routine job for that matter—asks us to build a fence around our deepest desires, our loftiest hopes, that dare us to pursue them.

I was angry at the rule that says in order to have a good life, you have to sacrifice your twenties, thirties, even forties, doing the shitty work that allows you to enjoy life later.

I was angry that I was spending the best eight hours of my day indoors, staring at a screen, instead of having the freedom to do what I wanted to do.

And I was angry that I was growing older by the second. Twenty months is a long time to sit at a desk drowning in data, especially when you have something you need to say; and I needed to say so much—about my family, about people, about the world. I wanted to showcase the things that were important to me, and to learn about the things I hadn't yet discovered. I desperately wanted to be heard, and it burned me up that something as pointless as scrolling through endless columns of numbers and crunching them to bits was keeping me from doing that.

But being angry about your life is a good thing, I realized, because it means you apparently love something else much, much more—even if you don't know yet what that something is. So the way I figured it, if I quit Venmo and traveled the world—if I took a great big breath and threw the dice on this crazy bet that I could hunt down and capture that "something else"—then maybe I'd be less angry.

I told my plans to Iqram Magdon-Ismail—he was Venmo's cofounder and the guy who'd originally hired me, so I thought I should let him know. He'd already left Venmo by then, but we'd stayed in touch. He was thrilled for me.

VENMO OFFICE, NEW YORK CITY

In fact, he'd been encouraging me all along to follow my dreams. "There are bigger and better things for you than staying in a job you don't want," he had told me. You don't get friends much better than that.

So I cleaned out my desk, turned in my badge, and walked out the door.

I don't recall exactly when the idea for Nas Daily was born. That's because it wasn't an aha moment—some divine crystallization of thought, when the sun broke through the clouds and the concept suddenly popped into my head. It was more like a slow burn, a gradual dawning, as I pieced together all of the bits of knowledge and experience I'd gathered in my previous endeavors.

The Rubik's Cube project had trained me in the art of speed-travel—how to jump from country to country, instantly connect with a culture (or at least try to), and share it all on video.

The Downtime app had taught me how to look for and deliver content that was precise and colorful—and, more important, could be condensed into sixty seconds.

My business studies at Harvard had instructed me how to reconcile the limitlessness of imagination with the cold, hard reality of budget.

And my upbringing in Israel had given me the most valuable lesson of all: that no matter what story you're trying to tell, it's all about the people. Always.

When I look back at the very first Nas Daily video I posted in April 2016, I have mixed feelings. Part of me cringes at my wide-eyed optimism and innocent enthusiasm, as if I considered this whole thing a lark—some harmless, two-month getaway that promised one video postcard a day and not much else.

"I have no clue why I'm doing this," I told the camera, "but I think it'll be fun! Once a day, I'm going to make one video that is one minute long. Coming with me are one drone, one heavy camera, one GoPro, Venmo tees, and protein bars. Let's do this!"

But on deeper reflection, I admire the honesty of that moment—because the fact is, I really *didn't* know what to expect; and I think by lowering the

DAY 1

bar that way, I was leaving myself the space to fail as many times as I needed to in pursuit of what they call in business school that perfect "product-market fit."

In other words, I knew there was an audience out there for what I had to offer. I just had to find it.

My nonchalance notwithstanding, I did have a few hard-and-fast rules that I intended to stick to—top among them, my commitment to making videos that were no longer than sixty seconds. As both a creator and consumer of online content, I knew that excessive length is a death sentence for any video—even footage of a tornado ripping across a wheat field gets boring after ten minutes. So I laid down the law: with rare exception, if I couldn't say it in a minute, I wouldn't say it at all. And my signature tagline—"That's one minute, see you tomorrow"—grew out of that.

Equally important was my decision to post one video a day. Not only did I know that any good product requires that kind of dedication and consistency, but I also knew that by keeping to that strict daily regimen, my work would get better.

I based this theory on that old story about a university professor who teaches a class about productivity by having the students make a vase. The professor divides the class into two groups and tells Group A to create as many vases as possible within the allotted forty-five minutes and tells Group B to make just one vase—but it has to be perfect.

Which group do you think makes the better vase? Group A, of course, because they had the most practice.

That's why I had to make videos daily. Some days, I didn't feel like picking up the camera; other days, I dove right in and came up with sixty seconds of shit. Everything is about process, and the only way I was going to become a better video maker—and a better storyteller—was by staying true to my 24-7 schedule.

Calling the show "Nas Daily" was also central to my concept for the series. I'd been given the nickname Nas six years earlier, when my freshman college roommate couldn't be bothered to pronounce my real name properly. "Nuseir is too hard to remember," he said, "so from now on you're 'Nas,' like the rapper." He had no idea, of course, that in Arabic, al-nas (الناس) means "people," yet the nickname stuck.

So it was only fitting that I adopted that name for the series—but not just as a gimmick. It ran deeper than that. From Day 1, I genuinely wanted viewers to see themselves—their own humanity, their own al-nas—through my eyes. Sure, I was the narrator of this epic travelogue, so naturally, my videos couldn't help but reflect my interests, my opinions, my curiosities, my passions. But if I was going to stay true to my guiding principle for the series—to make every day count, to live the best possible life, and to share it all on Facebook—I needed to make sure the people on the other side of the camera would be inspired to think about how they, too, could live their own best possible lives.

This took some time to get right. In the beginning, my videos focused too heavily on places—a random restaurant in Ethiopia, an underwhelming waterfall in India—and that wasn't going to cut it. If I wanted my videos to have meaning, I couldn't simply post a clip of me getting coffee on a nice beach. That's just vlogging—and I'm not a vlogger. I knew I had to connect with viewers in a more personal way.

On Day 52, I got a faint glimmer of that kind of connection. I was in Nepal, having just returned from a seven-day trip to the Himalayas, and I stopped in Kathmandu to grab footage of the wreckage there. Only thirteen months earlier, in 2015, a 7.8-magnitude earthquake had struck the central part of the country—flattening entire villages, killing nearly nine thousand people, injuring more than twenty-two thousand, and leaving hundreds of thousands homeless. Some of the more sorrowful damage befell Kathmandu Durbar Square, a UNESCO World Heritage Site, where several temples had collapsed.

I milled through the square, capturing the images of the destruction with minimal commentary, allowing the devastating pictures to speak for themselves.

When I posted the segment on Facebook that evening, one of the first viewer comments came from someone named Noppakorn Rajja, home country unknown, who wrote simply, "So heartbreaking. I hope you get well soon, Nepal." Next to the post was a little emoji of an angel.

KATHMANDU DURBAR SQUARE, 2016

It wasn't a particularly trenchant comment; it certainly wasn't wordy. But I instantly knew that somewhere on this planet, a person had been moved by what I had shared. He'd connected with the story. He'd *felt something*. And because he'd felt something, he was compelled to communicate his compassion to those who were suffering.

That meant a lot to me. Now, if only I could do that every day.

If I have one reservation about telling the story of Nas Daily in book form, it is that words alone cannot do justice to the exquisite artistry of my closest collaborator: my drone.

It wasn't until Day 4 of Nas Daily that I first launched my DJI Phantom 2 quadcopter—from a suburban soccer field in Nairobi, Kenya—and the images she sent back from that maiden flight were fairly routine. But she was just getting warmed up. In the ensuing one thousand days, my drone would take to the skies of nearly fifty countries on six continents, instantly flinging back startling portraiture of whatever slice of earth she had her expert eye trained on—from the electric-blue splendor of Italy's Amalfi Coast to the sparkling steel majesty of downtown Singapore.

As with most electronics, the more I used her, the better we both got at delivering the goods.

I launched her above the sprawl of the Xinyi business district in Taipei, and her renderings of the skyscrapered horizon were magnificent.

AMALFI COAST, ITALY

I sent her into the choppy air above San Francisco Bay on a long, slow loop around Alcatraz Island—at one and a half miles, her longest flight yet—and she returned home safely, out of breath but triumphant.

In fact, I was so confident of her skills that on Day 153, I pitted her against an Audi R8 sports car in a race through the Swiss countryside. She got her butt kicked.

During the first two years of Nas Daily, I replaced my drone twelve times, either when a newer and better model became available or when I trashed my existing one. The latter happened a lot. One slammed into a tree on a camping trip in Romania; another met her fate in Manhattan when I tied a pizza box to her tail, like a kite; and still another bought the farm in Greece, when I accidentally superglued her battery to her.

Oh, and a fourth one was attacked by a pit bull. He won.

But the greatest enemy of drones is not the weather or the terrain or even the fools who fly them—it's the governments that forbid them from doing their thing. Air bans were all too common during my Nas Daily travels. Morocco hates the little buggers, as do India, Turkey, and Japan. And the authorities around the Himalayas definitely have a problem with them.

"You have two options," a uniformed guard told me as I was about to begin my hike to Annapurna Base Camp. "You deposit your camera here and you go. Or you keep your camera and you go . . . out." I lost that battle.

I'd be less than honest if I didn't mention that, on several occasions throughout the series, I bent the law to get the shot—whether it was sneaking in a fast flight or piloting the drone above permissible limits—and I'm lucky to have eluded jail (though I did get detained three hours for unlawful droning in India). That said, there was one location where I voluntarily abstained from droning: the Syrian border. I may be an outlaw, but I'm not stupid.

So for all the trouble drones can stir up—and the expense they incur—why did I insist that a drone accompany me for nearly three years of daily travel? Because the world is more meaningful from above.

From ground level, Balicasag Island in the Philippines is lovely but ordinary. From thirteen hundred feet, it's a spellbinding, perfect oval.

That beach I visited in Costa Rica seemed like nothing special—until the drone revealed that it's shaped exactly like a whale's tail.

Standard footage of New Zealand's seventy-four million sheep is typically wall-to-wall wool—but with a drone, you see a flock as if God were the shepherd.

DRONING THE PLANET . . .

📍 BALICASAG ISLAND IN THE PHILIPPINES

📍 WHALE TAIL BEACH IN COSTA RICA

📍 SHEEP IN AUCKLAND, NEW ZEALAND

📍 ECONOMIC INEQUALITY ON THE STREETS OF BANGKOK

📍 SYRIAN REFUGEE LIFE VESTS IN LESBOS, GREECE (NAS AT CENTER)

📍 HIROSHIMA, JAPAN

But most important, the right aerials unveil for the viewer the very picture of our humanity—and sometimes inhumanity. A bird's-eye clip of a slum just across the alley from a luxury resort in Bangkok speaks to us about the shame of income inequality.

An overhead shot of modern-day Hiroshima drives home just how much damage was wrought when the atomic bomb was dropped on the city in 1945.

And though we know that far too many Syrian refugees risk death every day as they escape the horror of war over treacherous waters to try to reach Europe, their real numbers are brought into heartbreaking relief when you see thousands of their life vests from above, stacked high on a secluded mountaintop in Greece.

If story is king—which it most definitely is—then drone footage is queen.

A few words about this book.

When I was approached in January 2018 with the idea of creating a book version of Nas Daily, my response was three words long: "Sure—but how?" I shoot sixty-second videos. So unless publishing technology could figure out a way to embed tiny video screens into the pages of a book, I couldn't imagine how we'd put the magic of Nas Daily between two covers.

But then I remembered what the series is about. People. Cultures. Lives. Humanity. And all the fancy camerawork in the world wasn't going to top that. Those are the things that reached the hearts of Nas Daily viewers every day. And those are the stories I could tell.

With that decided, all that was left to figure out was how to spin the tale—an exercise not all that different from sitting in front of my laptop and cobbling together a Nas Daily video. Do we make the book a documentary travelogue? A personal diary? Or (God forbid) a guidebook? And even more pressing was the question of which adventures to tell you about. Nas Daily spent more than a thousand days on the road, so we knew we had some serious picking and choosing to do.

That's when we settled on the idea of compiling for you the most powerful things I learned while traveling the globe. Because the fact is, no matter where I went—from the sunny beaches of the Maldives to the moonlit forests of Papua New Guinea—I always walked away with some new lesson, some unexpected insight, tucked into my travel bag. I may be fifteen years older than that shy young boy cruising the internet from his bedroom in northern Israel, but I still want to learn something new every day. Nas Daily gave me that opportunity, and I'm so honored to share those lessons with you.

Also included in these pages is a bonus feature I introduced on Day 300 of Nas Daily. I called them "Nas Stories," and they spotlighted a particular person or place I thought deserved special mention. We picked the best of the best to share with you here. Additionally, many times during my travels, something prompted me to pause for reflection. Sometimes it was an off-camera experience that I wanted to explain; other times, it was something I'd been thinking about for a while and needed to unload. I've included some of those pieces here for you under the title "Nas Moment"—because the way I see it, a moment is different from a minute, even if it takes you just sixty seconds to say it.

The stories you're about to read have no predictable order or rigid chronology—that would take the fun away. For me, travel has never been about the planned destination, but rather the exhilaration of not knowing what's going to come your way. So I thought I would keep you guessing, too.

And the truth is, life is a lot more fun when you're kept guessing. As I write these words, I'm sitting in a plane, headed from the Maldives to Israel. I shot my final video for Nas Daily a few weeks ago, and all I know about the coming days is where I'll be staying. What happens next remains a sweet mystery.

But this I do know: I will be among friends, most of whom I've never met. This is, perhaps, the greatest gift of Nas Daily—I'm now greeted by new friends in every city I travel to. When I was still shooting the series, five hundred to a thousand people would show up just to say hello; now they spot me on the street and ask to take a selfie with me, which I'm always honored to do. It's such a wonderful rush to arrive in a city and instantly feel like a local—to feel like you *belong* everywhere in the world.

My journey began as one guy with a plane ticket, and ended up as a twelve-million-person celebration. This is my story.

BEFORE WE BEGIN

Over the course of a thousand days, I was often asked to explain a few details about the series. Here are a handful of the most commonly asked questions. Think of this as a preboarding procedure.

1. WHY DO YOU POST YOUR VIDEOS ON FACEBOOK INSTEAD OF YOUTUBE?

Because it's a better platform for what I do. For one thing, Facebook is a community of real people—unlike on YouTube, where you're not real. (Don't believe me? Ask Saddam Hussein—that's actually someone's name on YouTube.) On Facebook I can make real friends, meet locals, create better videos, get jobs, even find love. Also, 85 percent of YouTube views are from just 9 percent of its users, most of them bored teenagers, and a lot of them bullies. That's not the connection I'm trying to make.

Additionally, on YouTube, the concept of messaging doesn't exist. It's mostly a one-way street, where creators are the cool people and viewers are a degree below them, just consuming their content. Rarely do I see dialogue, interactions, or meetups—it's just someone talking, not a conversation. Facebook, on the other hand, mastered the art of messaging, and collaborations happen because of that. When I was on the road with Nas Daily, I didn't travel with fifty models and a film crew, so I needed people. Consequently, whenever I arrived in a new city, all I had to do was share a picture and write, "I just landed. Let's all meet tomorrow at noon!" The next day one hundred people would show up. It was a beautiful thing.

Don't get me wrong. YouTube piano tutorials are one of the reasons I got into Harvard. But I don't make tutorial videos.

2. HOW CAN YOU AFFORD TO TRAVEL SO MUCH?

It was different at the beginning because I was on a strict budget. Although I had savings from working two years in New York City, I'm basically a very cheap person, and I applied that cheapness to my travel. No fancy hotels for $200 a night, when a $10-a-night hostel is just fine, thank you. I also never splurged on lavish meals or clothes—and I definitely stayed away from Paris, which is crazy expensive. Ethiopia, India, Nepal, Nigeria—they're just as beautiful as Paris, if not more so, and they don't break your bank.

After about a year, when my subscriber base crossed into the millions, I started getting freebies from companies—airlines, hotels, tourism organizations—that were eager for the promotion, and I gratefully tagged them in the comments section on Facebook. But none of that required me to change the content of the videos—that remained sacred to me. What's priceless, and always will be, is the freedom to go to a random new country, find locals, and make friends. That's something you just can't buy.

3. WHAT DOES YOUR T-SHIRT MEAN?

On Day 200, I decided to celebrate that milestone by making a commitment to wearing the same T-shirt every day—one that explained the core philosophy of Nas Daily. To make it interesting, math was involved. I realized that at age twenty-four (and eight months), I was actually 32.4 percent old, once you factored in the average life expectancy of a male in the United States—which is 76.3 years. Being almost one-third done with my life was a pretty sobering statistic for me, but rather than ignore it, I decided to wear it on my chest as a constant reminder of the preciousness of life and how we choose to use that time. No way in hell was I going to spend ten years (13 percent) in a job I didn't like, or even two years (3 percent) in a relationship with someone I didn't love. Every single percentage of your life matters.

My friends Daniel Prosky and Candace Rogati came up with the design for the tee, and I loved it at first sight. It was thrilling to see real artists turn the thoughts that were swirling in my head into the perfect wash-and-dry, permanent-press expression of my feelings.

4. WHY DON'T YOU EVER VISIT MY COUNTRY?

Well, if you're in an Arab country, it's because I'm not allowed. As an Israeli citizen with an Israeli passport, I'm banned from visiting the majority of the Arab world—10 percent of the planet—even though I'm an Arab myself. It's pure politics, and it's ridiculous.

The visa process is also insane. At one point during the run of Nas Daily, I wanted to visit Australia, but at the time the government rejected my visa application because, according to them, I didn't have a job (even though visiting their country *was* my job). It took me four tries over the course of one year to convince them I'd be a courteous guest. And then, of course, there was the time I tried to book a flight from New York to India on Kuwait Airways, but, again, because I'm an Israeli, an entire airline was forbidden from taking me on its planes, even if I wasn't going to Kuwait. I fumed about that for weeks.

There was one country I managed to "visit" even though Israelis are banned from it. It took a little planning, but we pulled it off. You'll read about that in these pages.

So trust me, I'd love to come to your country, wherever you are. But if I'm not there, in all likelihood it's because of where my mother chose to give birth to me.

5. IN ALL YOUR TRAVELS, WHAT'S BEEN YOUR FAVORITE COUNTRY SO FAR?

It depends on when you ask me. On Day 157, it was Ethiopia, for its rich culture and mind-blowing nature; on Day 680, it was Morocco, for its sheer beauty—from the meticulously detailed architecture to the stunning food presentation. But the real answer is: no country is my favorite country. I was born a Palestinian and lived in Israel, so I never really had a strong connection to any nation or state. I moved to the United States not because it's the best country on the planet but because it's the best for what I wanted to do: tech. So as a rule, I tend to be a little wary of people who put their own country above the rest. History tells us that this often leads to discrimination and war. That's why Nas Daily celebrates the cultures that thrive around the world, and not just random geographical borders drawn by some king or politician centuries before we were born.

6. DID YOU EVER MISS A DAY OF NAS DAILY?

Never. Not once. Not even an afternoon. After two and a half years, I'm sure I would have been excused for calling in sick one day or taking the weekend off. But I stuck to my promise—even when I had the flu. Even when I was sleeping in the Amazon with no Wi-Fi. Even when I was in transit on some twenty-four-hour travel day, which happened all the time. I like to wear this accomplishment as a badge of honor, but there's an equally good argument that this is just unhealthy.

7. WHO IS THAT SMART, FUNNY, AND BEAUTIFUL WOMAN WHO HANGS OUT WITH YOU IN MANY OF YOUR VIDEOS?

I'm glad you asked. I had never planned to make Nas Daily a joint venture. I've always been kind of independent, and when I set out on this oddball mission, I assumed I'd be traveling solo.

I assumed wrong. On Day 58 I launched a video from Jerusalem, and almost immediately viewers began posting their comments. Among the reactions was one that read, "Hey! I love Jerusalem, too. Let's explore it together one day!"

I clicked on this stranger's Facebook profile and found her . . . alluring. We exchanged a few messages, and I took her up on her offer of friendship. Three days later, she joined my family and me in Arraba, on camera, as we celebrated the end of our Ramadan fast. She appeared in the next three videos and, seven weeks later, I joined her on a trip to Greece, where we toured the islands together with her cousins.

Then came Italy, Turkey and Jordan, the Azores and Portugal, Brazil and Malta, and many world locations in between.

That Alyne Tamir became an important part of Nas Daily was completely unexpected. But that didn't stop us from living our relationship out loud—on camera and in real time. We announced publicly that we were dating (Day 445) and, eleven months later, even asked our viewers if we should marry. They said yes; she said no.

You'll read a lot about Alyne in these pages, as she wove her story, our story, into the very fabric of Nas Daily. I'm not very good at writing about romance, so permit me to frame my feelings this way:

BAOBAB TREE IN MADAGASCAR

In May 2017, Alyne and I traveled to Madagascar together, where we spent fifteen hours driving to a remote location outside Morondava, for the singular purpose of seeing the legendary baobab trees—a rare and sacred species of tree that is steadily, sadly vanishing from the face of the earth. Most of the baobabs we saw that day stood tall and lonely in the arid soil—except for two of them that had grown entwined, hugging each other for centuries in the middle of a dying forest.

Whenever I watch that footage, I am reminded of why I embarked on this marvelous journey in the first place, and whose irreplaceable company I have cherished most.

THE WORLD'S MOST SENSITIVE TOPICS

In life, they say, there are three things you should never talk about in polite company: money, religion, and politics. And I've never quite understood why these topics are taboo.

I receive great pleasure from being transparent, because I believe that the more we talk about money, religion, and politics, the better our world will become. So here goes.

MONEY

To many people, the most sensitive question you can ask is, "How much money do you have?" Personally, I don't understand why that question might bother someone. Why do people hide the very thing they work their entire lives to make? So in the spirit of full disclosure, I'll take the first step and tell you about every cent I currently have:

As of this writing (January 2019), I have $950,000: $600,000 in cash and $350,000 in investments (in companies like Amazon, Tesla, and Apple; and in real estate holdings in Palestine, Sri Lanka, and the United States). Also, at this very moment, my wallet has a hundred bucks in it.

Also, I'm one of the cheapest people you'll ever meet.

This wasn't easy to disclose, but it's necessary to make my point. Although my net worth has very little correlation to who I am, I have just decided to become financially naked to millions of people. And when millions more become financially naked, too, the world will have a greater chance of becoming a more equal, fair, and transparent place.

I thought a lot about the upsides and downsides of making this disclosure, and the upsides won. That's because there are countless benefits to being financially transparent. Here are three:

1. If we all know how much the other person makes, the pay gap between men and women might not be as wide. Indeed, one of the reasons women get paid less than men is because they don't *know* that their male colleagues are getting more.

2. We all make better financial decisions with the help of friends, family, and advisors—and they can't help us if they don't know our financial status. I know this from personal experience.

3. Everybody worries about money, and that worry is usually bottled up. So the more we talk freely about our financial concerns, the more air we let out of our anxiety.

RELIGION

Religion is yet another sensitive topic. But, again, in the interest of transparency, let's roll:

I was born and raised Muslim. Growing up, I prayed five times a day, and for ten years straight I fasted during Ramadan. I was taught that Islam is the only way to heaven, and I believed it.

Then I started making non-Muslim friends.

The Christians said, "Jesus is the son of God, and he is the way to heaven."

The Jews said, "We are the chosen ones."

The Hindus said, "There is not only one god; there are millions."

And my atheist friends said nothing. (Okay, okay—they laughed at us.)

The more people I met, the more I noticed that everyone thinks their religion is right. And if their religion is right, it only makes sense that everyone else's is wrong—including mine.

As you can imagine, none of this sat well with me, and that's why I stopped believing in religion. I continued to believe in the idea of God, just not in the box he or she comes in. Don't get me wrong—religion is a wonderful thing for some people, and I may be religious again one day. But at this point in my life, before I sign on to one belief, I need to be convinced that all fingers point to the same moon.

Until that time comes, I've decided to look inward and become a better person. Instead of praying every day, I try to love myself and to love others with the fullness of my heart. And I hope that if there actually is a powerful being up there watching over us, he or she is also reading this book.

POLITICS

Believe it or not, this topic is the most sensitive of the three. I have come to learn this the hard way. And though I have no intention of turning this book into a political seminar, I have every intention of committing to full honesty:

I grew up in Israel as a Palestinian, and because of that, I never felt like I belonged to any country. In a world filled with political noise, the Middle East is the noisiest—and Israel is practically screaming. That's why when I watched Barack Obama win the American presidency in 2008—six thousand miles away, at 6:00 a.m. Israel time—I cried from excitement. And when Donald Trump became president eight years later, I cried for entirely different reasons.

If you've watched even a handful of my videos, it's no surprise to you that I'm a liberal and a progressive. I believe in globalism, in open borders, in gun control, in LGBTQ rights, and in universal health care.

I think Trump is a disaster.

But after my Nas Daily trip to Nebraska, I began to look differently at Trump voters. While I still didn't align with their politics—and especially their choice for leader of the free world—I grew to admire their love of family, their love of freedom, and their love of democracy.

The fact is, we the people—no matter where we live—are beholden to politics every day. As someone who spent his childhood in the hottest of global hot spots, I understand this in the most personal way. But I also believe that we complicate the problem by making discussions about politics, religion, or money verboten. As long as we learn to express our opinions civilly, why not share them with others? The worst thing that can happen is someone might change your mind.

PART 1

THE WORLD IS MUCH DIFFERENT THAN I THOUGHT

HOW INDIA BLEW MY MIND

When I was a kid, I wasn't very worldly. I knew only my immediate surroundings—my village, my country, and my family. So I would regularly wonder, *What's hiding in this world?* Now that I have traveled the globe for three years—a thousand days straight—I have the answer:

There are a lot of beautiful mountains in this world.

There are gleaming, magnificent cities.

There are millions of interesting and friendly people.

And there's a lot of poverty—a shockingly large amount of it.

Poverty is one of those words that's hard to define. We see pictures of it in our minds—dirty streets, run-down homes, beggars—but what truly makes a person impoverished? Who is poor and who is not?

Those definitions we leave to the experts. According to the World Bank, you are technically "extremely" poor if you live on less than $1.90 a day. I was surprised to read that. A dollar ninety is an alarmingly small amount of money to live on every day. And yet even with such a depressingly low number, would you believe that a full 10 percent of the people in the world live on

---

* I traveled to sixty-four countries over the course of one thousand days, sometimes returning to the same country for multiple visits. Although many of the essays in this book combine several trips, the dateline at the top of these stories refers to either the first day that Nas Daily visited a particular country or the day on which a specific video was posted.

even less than that? Thirty years ago, that number was 36 percent, so we're making progress. But still.

I would be lying if I said I could relate to extreme poverty. I can't. I grew up in a middle-class family in a developed nation. By global definitions, I was—and remain—rich. And you're rich, too. If you bought this book, that means you have enough disposable income to live above the poverty line. Extreme poverty is impossible to relate to unless you've lived it.

And because poverty is so far beyond our imaginations, we tend to stereotype it: The poor are lazy. They are dangerous. They don't work as hard as us, and they certainly aren't as enterprising. These stereotypes—as hurtful and untrue as they are—persist, even from the most well-meaning of us. And it takes something powerful to make us see things differently.

Enter India. That's where I got my first look at poverty. Real poverty. Slum poverty. I know that it's a cliché to say that a place can change you, but India changed me. India changes everyone.

That's because, among the civilizations of the world, India has always been a player. For one thing, it's pretty damn old. According to archaeologists, the earliest authenticated human remains in the region date back thirty thousand years. Today, more than one billion people inhabit that same patch of earth—1.3 million square miles of forests, valleys, and breathtaking mountains. And the people of India have permanently etched themselves

TAJ MAHAL IN AGRA, INDIA

into our civilization's history—from religion and philosophy to architecture and literature.

Today, a little bit of India is in all of us. If you take a yoga class, that's India. If you like the look of henna, that's India. And every time you button your shirt, you're hat-tipping India—because buttons were first used in the Indus Valley in 2000 BCE. Pretty cool, right?

Yet in that same country—right now, in 2019—21 percent of its citizens live below the poverty line. Slums are visible in every part of the land, from small townships to big cities. I'd seen these types of slums only in Hollywood movies, and like most people, I wasn't all that eager to visit them. But if you don't visit them, you don't know what goes on there.

I visited India twice during Nas Daily. The first time was on Day 19. Within minutes of exiting the airport, I saw a kind of poverty I'd never witnessed before. I'd read about the struggling parts of the country, but seeing them was different. Having made the decision to crawl inside the skin of the countries I visited—and not just take pretty pictures of them—I knew that in order to understand the challenges of the poor, I needed to spend a full twenty-four hours in India living below that World Bank figure of $1.90 (or 125 rupees) a day.

It wasn't easy. In fact, I was astonished by how many hard choices I was forced to make. Skip breakfast. Walk whenever possible. Look for public drinking fountains rather than spend 20 rupees on bottled water. Think twice before spending money on a bus fare. Think three times before buying food. It was mentally exhausting to live within such a tiny budget. I slept that evening on the hard tile floor of a church. "Thank God for organized religion," I told my viewers, only half-jokingly.

Enter Mumbai—the capital of the country, its most populous city, and one of the top-ten centers of commerce and finance in all the world. I was mesmerized by the city's sheer magic, from the twinkle of its evening skyline to the street-corner food vendors shaving ice for sweet pops, or grilling corn, or carving large strips of lamb and chicken for the shawarma that tourists love.

But then I climbed onto a tour bus that puttered through the city's choked streets and took me to Dharavi, a tiny municipality that sits smack in the middle of this thriving metropolis.

What a difference. With nearly a million people squeezed into less than one square mile of littered streets, open sewers, and tiny, decrepit hovels, Dharavi is, at first glance, the very face of poverty and, in fact, the largest

MUMBAI, INDIA

slum in Asia. And I'd done my homework. I'd read about the city's sanitation problems. I knew that, statistically, there was just one toilet for every five hundred people, and that residents suffered a host of diseases, more than 80 percent of them waterborne.

I saw the destitution with my own eyes; and had I been a different kind of videographer, I might have left after an hour or so with enough footage to make the case that this was a city beyond hope.

But I didn't leave. I walked deeper into Dharavi, poked into shops, tapped on doors, and asked if I could come in. I spent hours exploring, and what I found blew my mind.

This slum, where you would expect to see nothing but the dark gloom of deprivation and misery, actually has an economy that generates up to $1 billion a year. A year! Workers toil around the clock in small manufacturing units that produce leather goods, embroidered garments, pottery, and plastics—an "informal economy," they call it.

Yes, I saw filthy alleyways, but inside people's homes I saw remarkable cleanliness—and the constant scrubbing of floors and washing of windows.

Yes, I saw the jobless—as you see in any city—but I also saw thousands of women and men, young and old, participating side by side in what appeared to be a robust labor force.

One by one, my preconceived notions of what constitutes a slum fell to the side. Dharavi was not a hotbed of violence and crime, as I had been warned. Instead, I saw a little town where people looked out for each other. At all times, I felt safe.

This was not a city of the disengaged and uneducated. The people I met there were sharp and friendly. Indeed, Dharavi lived up to its reputation as the most educated slum in all of India, with a literacy rate of 69 percent.

I saw the slum community up-close, and I am not exaggerating when I say I struggled to find someone who wasn't hard at work. I walked into a cramped recycling factory, where workers tackled a mountain of empty plastic jugs that towered above us.

I walked the floors of pottery and leather studios, where the employees looked more like artists than assembly-line workers.

My entire concept of a slum was demolished in a single day—and that's usually the way it is with stereotypes, isn't it? That's why it's so important to challenge those stereotypes when you travel anywhere. It's so easy to see a place and its people the way they might appear in the guidebooks. But if you can get past that—if you can do the *real* work of travel, living the culture from inside of it—the surprises and the rewards are immeasurable.

DHARAVI, INDIA

At dusk, I hopped into a rickshaw and left Dharavi, headed for my hotel. As the bustle of the little town faded behind us, I thought back on my day and concluded one thing about what I'd just experienced: that the poor people of Dharavi work harder than I do, are more creative than I am, and are more enterprising than I will ever be. They possess the same work ethic and durable spirit that I so admire in the United States. It just happens that they live in a place we call a "slum."

I HAD A DREAM

CANADA, DAY 906

When I was a child, what I wanted more than anything in the world was the American Dream. From the earliest age, I was hell-bent on immigrating to the United States because, in my eyes, it was the only country on the planet that gets it.

The only country with opportunities for everyone.

The only country where you can make it big.

And the only country that embraced immigrants.

But now that I'm a bit older and a bit wiser, I realize I may be wrong.

CANADA HAS 31,752 LAKES—THE MOST ON THE PLANET

Don't get me wrong: the American Dream is objectively great. In fact, I'm living it at this moment. I've got my American visa, I'm building my American company, and I'm sharing my life with a woman who was born in Los Angeles, schooled in Utah, and is, in many ways, an all-American girl (with a dash of Israeli thrown in).

But the kid in me was wrong in thinking that the United States is the only place on earth with a dream.

Enter Canada.

When it comes to superlatives, Canada's rap sheet is pretty damn impressive: At nearly four million square miles, it's the second largest country in the world (after Russia). It also boasts the longest coastline (150,000 miles), the longest binational land border (with the United States), the most lakes on the planet (31,752 of those babies), and some seriously extreme climate. In 1937, temperatures shot up to 113 degrees in Yellow Grass, Saskatchewan; then ten years later, it dropped to –80 in the Yukon. That's harsh.

What's not often listed on Canada's CV, however, is that it has a Canadian Dream.

I visited Canada toward the end of my Nas Daily journey, with the intention of spending just a few days there before flying off to Europe. I wound up staying for nearly two weeks. That's because I discovered that, over the course of its colorful history, Canada has built a nation that the kid in me dreamed of living in. A nation that loves immigrants, a nation with opportunity, and a nation that thrives on community.

Case in point: In 2017, Canada's new Minister of Immigration, Refugees, and Citizenship, Ahmed Hussen, proudly announced that the country would be welcoming nearly one million immigrants over the next three years. To those who were listening, that was a true sign of Canada's famously open arms to the people of the world.

Well, here's the kicker: Hussen himself is an immigrant. Born and raised in Mogadishu, Somalia, he lived through the Somali Civil War in the 1980s, then relocated with his family to a refugee camp in Kenya. When he was seventeen, his parents sent him to Toronto, where his brothers had already relocated. And within seven years, he'd begun a celebrated career in politics and public service, ultimately becoming the first Somali minister in Canada's history. All by itself, the story of Minister Hussen screams opportunity.

THE TORONTO PUBLIC LIBRARY: BOOKS AND A WHOLE LOT MORE

I met the minister at a citizenship ceremony in a government building in Halifax, Nova Scotia. Outside, the weather was cold and cloudy; but inside, the warmth of humanity was palpable. Here were people from all around the globe—India, Pakistan, the Philippines, Somalia, and the United States—each of them bursting with pride at becoming citizens of a country they had not been born into but *chose* to be part of.

And the idea that this precious honor was being bestowed on them by none other than the refugee-turned-minister himself was one of the most beautiful moments of inclusion and diversity I have ever seen. My eyes welled up when everyone in the room sang the Canadian national anthem. And afterward, the Honorable Hussen spoke to Nas Daily's camera, reminding us all, "In Canada, diversity is our strength, and inclusion is our choice."

While I was in Toronto, I also had the privilege of meeting Jim Estill, a technology-entrepreneur-turned-philanthropist who in 2015 threw a fifty-seven-hundred-mile lifeline to eighty-seven families fleeing war in Syria. Worried about the crisis, Jim took advantage of Canadian laws that permit private sponsorship of refugees and singlehandedly brought over three hundred Syrian refugees to live in Canada.

"It's the most fulfilling thing I've ever done," Jim told me, adding that even though it cost him a couple million dollars—out of his own pocket—the decision was a no-brainer. "Doing the right thing. How tough can that be?"

Jim was ultimately awarded national medals—including the Order of Canada—for his philanthropy, but he pointedly noted that you don't need to be a millionaire to do the same thing. On average, he told me, it costs $30,000 to sponsor a family of four or five for one year, so groups of ten people can pitch in and pay for a sponsorship for as little as $3,000 each. At the time, Canada was just one of three countries in the world that permitted private refugee sponsorship (Britain and Argentina were the other two), but the trend was beginning to spread.

Either way, Jim and I did disagree on one thing: he called himself "just a guy." I called him Superman.

As if meeting Jim and Minister Hussen hadn't already persuaded me that Canada is an exceptionally cool place to live, I got another big dose of the country's charms in, of all places, the library.

Canadian libraries have been hailed not only for their stunning architecture (from the beaux arts to the modern) and their impressive collections (the Bibliothèque et Archives nationale du Québec stores historic documents dating back to the seventeenth century), but for their passionate devotion to educating patrons in ways that go beyond turning the pages of a book. I spent the day in the Toronto Public Library and didn't want to leave. Once I got past the eye-popping interior design—which looked like a cross between a fancy mall and the International Space Station—I marveled at the breadth of its facilities: endless banks of computers, 3-D printers, conference rooms, puppet-show stages, art rooms, a video production studio (complete with green-screen), and a full-scale replica of Sherlock Holmes's study—including his books!

But that wasn't even the half of it. What blew me away were the library's onsite courses, which in my short visit included classes in knitting, shoemaking, painting, public speaking, and sushi preparation. This hands-on care doesn't stop when you walk out the door. If you need assistance getting the little ones to wind down at night, you can call the library's Dial-a-Story hotline, which delivers bedtime stories to sleepless tots in sixteen languages.

And did I mention all of this is for free?

Looking after kids is a priority in Canada, and I saw this up-close when I dropped in on a day-care center in Quebec, which offers gold-standard, universal daytime childcare for kids ages four and younger. Subsidized by the government, day care in Quebec is the best in the nation, costing parents only $7.30 to $20 per day—a real steal compared with the skyrocketing prices in the United States. More than just saving costs, it allows young parents to return to work without worry after the birth of their children, while offering crucial support to low-income families for whom holding a steady job is everything.

Granted, the topic of government-subsidized day care has ignited a lot of debate both inside and outside of Canada—some love it, some don't—but what matters is that the country is taking a bold step toward making life easier and more affordable for families, while helping the country maintain a healthy labor force.

Before leaving Canada, I had to make one more stop at a very special spot—a place, I think, that speaks to the true heart of the Canadian. I'd read about it in the news, but I needed to see it with my own eyes. It was a quiet airport.

On September 11, 2001, as the world reeled in horror from the terrorist attacks in New York, Washington, DC, and rural Pennsylvania, American airspace was immediately shut down for security reasons. Consequently, incoming flights were redirected to the international airport in the tiny town of Gander on the northeastern shores of Newfoundland. The selection of Gander International for the diversion was based on two factors: its ability to land large aircraft, and the fact that it wasn't in a large metropolitan area—like Toronto or Montreal—which might have been targets for additional attacks.

In total, 38 airliners, including 6,122 passengers from 95 countries and 473 crew members, landed at Gander, which was suddenly charged with providing food, shelter, and security for its exhausted and disoriented guests.

The entire town—with a population of about ten thousand—and the surrounding fishing villages instantly mobilized. They turned homes, churches, schools, and community centers into pop-up dormitories for the "plane people," providing them with food, clothing, toiletries, and computers.

GANDER INTERNATIONAL AIRPORT IN NEWFOUNDLAND, CANADA

Hospital and bakery staffs pulled extra shifts, while the local hockey rink was transformed into a giant walk-in refrigerator.

The town's school bus drivers—who had been on strike at the time—left their picket lines to join the effort, which was dubbed Operation Yellow Ribbon.

Even the animals that were on board the planes—seventeen dogs and cats and two chimpanzees that had been on their way to the Columbus zoo—were taken under the wing of Gander's guardian angels.

The plane people ultimately began making their way home after four days, all of them permanently touched by the town that had cared for them. Two of the stranded passengers had fallen in love and eventually married. A gay couple who had planned to move to a small town in Canada but worried that they wouldn't be accepted were now worry-free. In those four days, Gander had changed their lives.

And yet none of the townspeople would accept money for their generosity. Like Jim Estill, they were simply doing the right thing.

"September 11 will live long in memory as a day of terror and grief," Canadian Prime Minister Jean Chrétien said on the first anniversary of the attacks. "But thanks to the countless acts of kindness and compassion done for those stranded visitors here in Gander . . . it will live forever in memory as a day of comfort and of healing."

From its people to its airports, from its government to its immigration laws—and yes, even inside its libraries—Canada has proven to be a welcoming place for all humans. And my short visit to this marvelous country convinced me that the Canadian Dream should be right up there next to the American one.

THE COUNTRY
I COULDN'T FIND
ON A MAP

A world map shows 195 independent countries. But here's a question: How many of those 195 countries can you actually find on that map?

Personally speaking, I'd have to say not many. Like millions of people, I can pinpoint only select countries—the big, shiny, developed ones, or the ones that impact my life: the United States, because I follow its elections (and I live there); the United Kingdom, because I'm interested in Brexit; Germany, for its football; and Australia, because, well, if I can't find Australia on a map, I have no business writing this book.

And, of course, I know every inch of the Middle East, from sea to embattled sea.

The rest of the gang? I never really paid attention.

Until July 2018. That's when I decided to visit a country that slipped through my radar. A country I hadn't heard much about. A country that even my friends didn't know existed.

That country is Armenia, and I went there specifically to see a place I'd ignored for most of my life.

That lesson began on my flight there, as I pored over my research on Armenia's history. Talk about your scrappy countries—this place seems to have spent its entire existence under someone else's thumb. In the twelfth century, it was conquered by the Mongols; then, three hundred years later, it was chopped in half by the ruling Ottomans and fought over for the next century by rival superpowers. In modern times, Armenia's fate continued to be dictated by larger forces beyond its control, and only in 1991, with the dissolution of the Soviet Union, did the country gained its independence. Whoa.

Those who can't find Armenia on the map are forgiven, as the country is practically hidden in the southern Caucasus, surrounded on all sides by Turkey, Georgia, Azerbaijan, and Iran. But during my twelve days in this land of snowcapped mountains, rushing rivers, and colorful urban bustle, I was less interested in Armenia's geography than I was in its intoxicating personality. It's the kind of place that screams, "We are unique, we are different—we do things *our way*."

And I was there to observe, to learn, to report.

I started with the water. On first arriving in Armenia's capital city of Yerevan, I immediately noticed a public water fountain on a boulevard sidewalk—three feet tall, carved from stone, with a pretty, graceful spout. No biggie, right? But then I noticed an identical fountain next to it. Then a few differently designed ones down the street. Then a cluster of them on the

ARMENIAN *PULPULAK*

next block. And on they went, street after street, block after block, fountain after fountain.

WTF?

So I asked around. Turns out that in 1968, in commemoration of the 2,750th birthday of Yerevan's ancient Erebuni Fortress, the city was gifted with 2,750 drinking fountains, which half a century later still serve thirsty and over-heated passersby around the clock. Watching the procession of fountain folk was a joyful experience, as each one—young or old, local or visitor—performed the identical routine, as if choreographed: approach the fountain, stop, stoop, sip, and move along. There was something almost poetic in its simplicity.

The locals call the fountains *pulpulak* (Armenian for "water source"), but I call them a genius system that reduces water waste through recycling, disposes of eco-unfriendly plastic bottles, and keeps everyone in the city—including the birds—well-hydrated. For free.

And if the drinking fountains aren't charming enough, there are the dancing fountains in Yerevan's Republic Square, the gold-lit complex of government buildings and museums that sits at the center of the city. Republic Square is a comforting gathering spot for longtime residents of this unassuming country, like a giant rec room, where night after night they congregate—laughing, talking, dancing. I hung out there a lot.

Over the next ten days, I would notice time and again how the Armenian culture seems less concerned with striking a pose for its competitive global neighbors than it is with looking inward to ensure the education, welfare, and happiness of its people. Kids, for example, are taught chess in school alongside their other mandatory courses in math and science. In some ways, this is to be expected: chess has been popular in Armenia since the early Middle Ages, and the game was institutionalized when Armenia was under Soviet rule. But in recent years, the country has amped up its commitment to chess, thanks in large part to a handful of world championships and a few homegrown grand masters—including Levon Aronian, who has become the Michael Jordan of the chessboard to children around the country.

But chess is more than just a game for these girls and boys. It's a way for them to learn how to focus, to compete, to develop patience and discipline and cognitive skills in preparation for adulthood. I spent a day in one of these chess classrooms and have never felt such brainpower coming out of people so small.

Like any country, Armenia is not without its problems. On my sixth day there, I traveled with a group of soldiers and specialists to the mountainous highlands of Nagorno-Karabakh, where they continue to search for and detonate the thousands of unexploded mines that were laid in the region in the early 1990s during Armenia's war with Azerbaijan. The protective gear we wore on our expedition—bright-blue safety vests and heavy plastic face visors—were small comfort, considering the explosive peril around us. I was reminded all over again about the many hidden costs of warfare around the globe—destroyed infrastructures, demolished schools, unexploded mines—and how, even when peace comes, war never ends.

When I flew out of Armenia, I was awash in all sorts of feelings. For one thing, I was embarrassed that just two weeks earlier, I'd known nothing about this remarkable, fiercely independent nation. I felt gratitude at having been welcomed so warmly to a country with such a rich and important history: the first to officially adopt Christianity, the first to build a cathedral (Etchmiadzin, 303 CE), and one of the oldest civilizations on the planet—even older than ancient Rome.

But mostly, I felt hope. Here is a country that holds fast to its past while keeping its eyes trained on the future—a place that sends its kids, after school, to modern institutions of learning, where they're taught engineering and design and music so that they can become grand masters in whatever they choose to pursue. Entirely for free.

A place that invests in technology companies that will keep the country on the cutting edge of global science and invention.

A place that quietly redefines the word *superpower*, focusing not on ephemeral things like Olympic medals or GNP, but instead on the strength and endurance of its people.

And a place where the national pride is among the most potent I've ever witnessed. When the president of Armenia, Armen Sarkissian, hosted our Nas Daily team at his offices, he toasted to the good fortune of all of us, with a large brandy snifter in his hand.

"Cheers with Armenian brandy!" he said, clinking his glass with ours, "the best in the world!"

THE HIDDEN SECRET OF MAPS

World maps are not accurate.

It's true. When I first learned this unsettling bit of news, I was shocked. The map we studied in school was drawn by a sixteenth-century German-Flemish cartographer named Gerardus Mercator. You can find that map online—it's still everywhere. If you take a look at Africa on the Mercator projection, as it's called, you'll see that the country is a respectable size—but swing your eyes to the west and check out Canada. Whoa! That mother could kick Africa's ass in a street fight, with one peninsula tied behind its back. As you'll also note, Russia and the United States are pretty big, too; Greenland is roughly the same size as Africa; and Antarctica is a monster that dwarfs the whole lot.

Now check out another map called the Gall-Peters projection. This one's a more accurate depiction of the world that was first introduced in 1855, but it took 125 years to start popping up in classrooms.

My, Africa—how you've grown! And Greenland? You can fit sixteen of those babies inside Africa and still have room for a coffee table. This actually makes total sense to me at the moment, because Alyne and I spent fifteen hours on a bus today, crossing a country we thought was the size of a shoe—Madagascar—but we just kept on going and going.

So why the discrepancy? Well, the technical reason was an innocent mistake. Mercator made the original map as a globe; but when it came time for him to transfer it to a flat piece of paper, the poles didn't look right, so he stretched them to fit nicely. (Photoshoppers will know what I mean.) It looked great, but in the process, North America and Europe went up a couple of dress sizes. But that didn't bother sixteenth-century people because they lived in Europe.

Yet the real problem with the Mercator projection is that it unfortunately reflects a political agenda that speaks to us more about ethnography than geography. By fattening up the Northern Hemisphere the way he did, Mercator—and the mapmakers who followed him—were fostering the ongoing presumption that the real power in the world is in the hands of the Anglo-Euro-American nation-states, which led to things like colonialism and empire-building.

Do we still possess that mindset today? Probably. Having traveled to more than sixty countries for Nas Daily, I can tell you that American and European influences dominate the globe—all you have to do is look for a Starbucks when you deplane. There's usually one in the airport. But coffee shops aren't the problem—nation-building is. That's why I'm glad to see the Gall-Peters projection being used more and more in classrooms these days. It proves in the deftest of ways that, yes, sometimes size matters.

By the way, I didn't know any of this stuff before this morning. But when you have fifteen hours to kill in the back of a bus, you look for interesting things to read.

I had come to Mexico to shine a light on the lives of its people, but on Day 532 I was drawn into the shadows of death in the lakeside town of Xochimilco, just south of Mexico City. It was among the tangled canals there that I drifted up to the lily-padded Isla de las Muñecas (Island of the Dolls), which I quickly dubbed "the scariest place in Mexico." Here's the spooky backstory: According to legend, more than fifty years ago the caretaker of the island, Julián Santana Barrera, discovered the body of a dead girl floating in the water; she'd drowned after getting snagged in vines while swimming. After her body was taken away, Julián found the girl's doll, and in a gesture of respect for the departed child, he hung it from a tree at the spot where she'd died. Alone in his hut, Julián began hearing the moans and footsteps of the dead girl, a taunting message that her soul was not at rest. So to appease her unhappy spirit, he began draping more and more dolls from the surrounding trees—hundreds of broken and discarded dolls he found on the island, many of them missing limbs and eyes and hair. At night, he swore he heard them whispering to each other and even saw them move. Julián died in 2001—he was found in the exact spot where the young girl had drowned—and today the Isla de las Muñecas has become a cult attraction for visitors from around the world. Some bring their own dolls and hang them with the others among the cobwebs. If I look frightened in the video I shot there, that's because I was.

JAPAN HE MADE A TALKING TRANSLATOR

Takuro Yoshida founded his first business as a teenager, dipping dried roses into gold paint and selling the shiny flowers online to men who were looking to gift their significant others. (He targeted male shoppers, he told me, by running the search terms "Girlfriend. Present. Expensive.") That's how Takuro made his first $200,000—which financed a new life for him in the United States. And it was there that he came

up with his next great brainstorm—quite by accident. He was standing at the counter at a Taco Bell, where he wanted to order a drink. But he suddenly grew embarrassed that he couldn't pronounce the word *water*. Rather than slink away in shame, Takuro—like many great inventors before him—turned personal calamity into professional triumph. Back home at his desk, he began sketching out his ili Translator—a sleek, off-line, handheld device that does your speaking for you. And it couldn't be easier to operate. Say a word or phrase into it in your own language, and a fetching female voice says it back to you instantly—in English, Japanese, Mandarin, or Spanish. And because it's internet-independent, you can use it anywhere—even at Taco Bell. Now that's ingenuity—in any language!

THE UNITED STATES
THE OTHER AMERICA

The only things I knew about Nebraska were Warren Buffett and corn. As an immigrant who'd settled in Boston and New York, I realized I carried biases about the flyover states; and as a liberal, I didn't expect to have much in common with them. So I decided to dispel those assumptions by booking a flight to a city where I had zero friends: Omaha. And I'm glad I did. True, you can drive for hours and hours in Nebraska and be surrounded by nothing. But in the middle of that nothing, I found something. I found Derek, who took me dirt-biking. I found O.J., who took me target-shooting. I found Payton, who took me night-flying. And I found Mark, the highway patrolman—or rather he found me. But just like any Nebraskan, he gave me a warm smile as he handed me my $250 speeding ticket. I'll be honest: I was a little skeptical when I'd woken up that first morning in a cheap hotel room by the highway; but during my four days in America's heartland, I found a welcoming posse who, like sixty-five million other Middle Americans, shared with me their homes, their religion (Cornhuskers football), their politics (we'll skip that), and their way of life. Without people, there is nothing in New York City. And with people, there is everything in Nebraska.

PERU THE BOILING RIVER

Big confession: I'm officially a poacher. But before you toss this book away in disgust, let me explain. On Day 986, Alyne and I dove deep into the Peruvian Amazon, a trek that required four hours of driving, canoeing, and hiking. Our destination was a shaggy patch of forest region called Mayantuyacu, and it was there that we witnessed a natural phenomenon that has baffled humanity for millennia: a boiling river. Four miles long and sixteen feet deep, the river—known as Shanay-Timpishka ("boiling with the heat of the sun")—is hotter than any bath you've ever taken, reaching temperatures as high as 200 degrees Fahrenheit. That's sizzling enough to give you third-degree burns if you fall into it—and it does indeed incinerate small animals who make the mistake of taking a dip. Ordinarily, water this toasty is the result of volcanic activity, but the nearest volcano is four hundred miles away. So what gives? There are competing theories. Peruvian legend has it that the roiling river is watched over by a giant serpent-spirit called Yacumama ("Mother of the Waters"), who turns the thermostat on and off at will; and local shamans believe the river has healing powers. But scientists have a more practical (though somewhat killjoy) hypothesis: the river is actually glacier water that gets nuked at the center of Mother Earth and then seeps back up through the cracks to create nature's own Jacuzzi. As for my confession: I tested the water to see whether it was hot enough to poach an egg. It was.

SENEGAL HE WANTED TO BE BLACK

I'd just finished my salad at the LuLu Home Interior & Café, a sweet little joint in Dakar, Senegal, when the shop's manager and executive chef, Clément Suleiman, revealed the strangest thing to me: "I always wanted to be black," he said. That's when Clément—who is white—told me his story. As a child in Belgium, he so deeply believed he was black that he painted his skin. His mom found this odd, so she took him to see a psychologist.

But rather than try to convince the kid that he wasn't black, the shrink advised Clément's mom to take him on vacation to Africa. So at age thirteen, Clément traveled to Senegal and never looked back. He went on to become a citizen there, learn all five of the country's local dialects, open a business, marry a Senegalese woman, and have two kids with her. "And now," Clément told me,

"I'm finally happy." It took me a few days to decide to tell Clément's story on Nas Daily. As an Arab who grew up feeling American—and then actually put down roots in the United States—I could totally relate. But race is different from citizenship; it's one thing to want to be black, but it's another to live inside black skin. I mustered the courage to post the video, if for no other reason than to start a discussion—and one indeed ensued. "Everybody wants to be black until the police show up," posted one follower. "The human soul has no color," countered another. My takeaway was slightly different: Clément will never truly be black, but he's a proud example of how home is not necessarily where and how you are born, but rather the place that makes you feel comfortable inside. It's all about belonging.

PART 2
THE STRUGGLE

MY BIGGEST SURPRISE

THE PHILIPPINES, DAY 272

I have learned that the easiest way to communicate—whether I'm standing in front of a camera or sitting at a keyboard, writing—is with complete honesty. So I'm going to be totally honest: before embarking on my Nas Daily journey, there were several countries I had very little interest in. No diss intended; that's just the way it was. As much world news as I devour every day, there is a limit to my curiosity.

The Philippines was one of those countries that didn't interest me. At all. In fact, in December 2016, just a month before boarding my flight there, it was among those places I couldn't even find on the map.

But the thing was, I kept getting invited there! Nas Daily was only in its ninth month when the messages began rolling into my in-box:

Come to the Philippines!
You won't believe it here!
This place is perfect for you!

And on and on. *They can't all be wrong*, I thought. So after ignoring about a hundred of these sweet invites, I finally buckled under and bought my ticket. And from the moment my plane touched down at Ninoy Aquino International Airport in Manila on Day 272, I was hooked. In fact, I fell so deeply, and so quickly, under the spell of this magic South Pacific nation that I spent the longest single stretch there of any country I visited during Nas Daily—five weeks and four days, to be precise.

There was a reason for that. Actually, there were several reasons, not the least of which is: it's an awesome place.

Composed of 7,107 developing islands (depending on who you ask), the Republic of the Philippines dominates the fifteen hundred miles of ocean that lies between mainland China to the north and Indonesia to the south. Its topography reflects that breadth, ranging from volcanoes and rainforests to manicured beaches and villages. I like things that surprise me, and no matter where you turn in the Philippines, your eye is always grabbed by something unexpected—from the rainbow-colored rooftops of Cebu City to the tree-jumping monkeys in the Chocolate Hills of Bohol Island.

And yet the real lure of the country—the thing that swept me off my feet—was the Filipino smile, which is like no other I've ever seen. It's hard to explain if you've never been on the receiving end of one, but the Filipino smile is a potent combination of kindness, cheer, and sincerity. I got one from the airport security guard, just seconds after I stepped off the plane. And then from the guy at the SIM card store. And then from the desk clerk at my hotel. Even the Uber driver smiled at me.

THE ISLANDS OF THE PHILIPPINES

Having just left Europe, I wasn't used to such contagious happiness, and at first I was flattered by it (*They already like me!* I thought). But after a while, I realized it had nothing to do with me. Filipino people, as I quickly came to learn, are by their nature some of the friendliest and most welcoming people on the planet.

So this was one of the first things I explored in the country. I decided to do one of my little social experiments to see how deeply that Filipino smile runs. On my fifth day there, I announced to my viewers that I would spend one full day in Manila on zero dollars. This was a

MANILA ON ZERO DOLLARS A DAY

variation on the experiment I'd done in India, when I lived on $1.90 for a full day. But in India, I was trying to experience poverty from the inside; in the Philippines, I was attempting to see just how far I could go, living off the generosity of complete strangers.

I wasn't sure it would work, but I gave it my best. I left my wallet in my room and hit the streets with no money.

It wasn't easy. By midmorning, I was already thirsty, so I began wandering the sidewalks in search of something to drink. That's when I spotted a uniformed guard unloading a truck of water-cooler bottles outside an office building. I approached him and gestured to the bottles.

"Is this water?" I asked. I had pointedly chosen those words because I didn't want him to think I was asking for a handout—that would ruin the experiment. The guard looked over at me and saw that I was Middle Eastern—just like him—and he must have detected that I was thirsty.

"Yes, this is water," he said. And then he handed me a small bottle of it.

"You are Muslim and I am Muslim," he said. "When people are thirsty, it is much better to give."

I was elated. This was actually working.

The same thing happened when I got hungry. I found a food cart on a street corner and told the vendor that I'd lost my wallet. He didn't respond, so I walked away. Suddenly, a young man who had been standing next to us chased me down the block, brought me back to the cart, and bought me a plate of noodles for $1.30. He told me that he'd been jobless, but that he'd just found work that morning—for $8 a day.

"I want to share my blessing with you," he said. I was speechless. After I turned my camera off, I offered to pay him back later, but he wouldn't accept any money. Apparently, sharing his blessing was all he really wanted.

And on it went like that, throughout the day, one gracious encounter after another. But as the sun began to set, I knew that I was about to face my biggest challenge. Freebie food and water is one thing, but lodging for the night is serious business. So I began outright asking people on the street for help.

"I lost my wallet and I can't find any nearby hotels!" I said, with a slight edge of panic in my voice. "I'm stranded." A handful of people passed by me—seven, to be exact—and then finally one young man caught my desperation.

"What happened to you, man?" he asked.

"It's a long story," I said.

He paused for a moment, then cheerfully offered his home to me. I couldn't believe it. He first took me to a food stand and bought me dinner; then he escorted me back to his flat. He gave me his bed for the night—he slept on the floor—and asked for nothing in return. He didn't even want to be filmed for the video I was making. Instead, he simply asked me to support his friend's charity, a nonprofit that helps Filipino educators, which I immediately promoted with a link when I posted the video.

As I drifted to sleep that night in this stranger's bed, I got teary-eyed thinking about the kindness and decency I'd been experiencing all day. It confirmed to me that, yes, there is still good in this world—but it also made me look inward. And if I was going to be truly honest with myself, I had to admit that I don't have that kind of giving mentality—or, at least, enough of it. Like the majority of the people I know, I make more than $8 a day. But have I ever chased someone down the street to "share my blessing"? Not even once.

I learned a lot from my experiment that day. I learned how to look for the humanity in others—something we often don't recognize right away—but I also thought about ways I could develop a similar kind of compassion in my own life. It was a humbling experience.

And the most remarkable thing is, this kind of generosity isn't so easy for many Filipinos—not because it doesn't come naturally to them, but because helping others costs money; and in the Philippines, the country's poverty rate lingers at around 20 percent. This is one of the reasons I stayed so long in the country. I had gone there, I assumed, to enjoy the beautiful islands, the tropical climate, and the famously cheap prices. But once I became confronted by the country's poverty, that reality hit hard. And the more I saw of it, the more I kept extending my trip.

The turning point happened when I visited Smokey Mountain.

Located in the densely populated coastal district of Tondo in northwestern Manila, Smokey Mountain is a towering dump site, sixteen stories tall, built from more than two million tons of urban waste—from bottles and tires to plastics, wood, and metals. At one point, more than twenty-five thousand people lived along the perimeter of this polluted three-and-a-half-mile landfill, where they spent their days picking up—and selling—garbage. Its nickname comes from the chronic tire fires that once blazed there, and it has often been called one of the most desperate and impoverished slums on the planet.

According to travel writers who have visited Smokey Mountain—and, yes, you can arrange tours there—residents of this hell on earth depend on the garbage to survive. Early in the morning, they are already awaiting the trucks that stream into the village, carrying thousands of pounds of waste from around Manila. Even before the trucks have pulled to a stop, residents have hopped aboard the dump bed and begun picking through the garbage for anything—a plastic water bottle, a tire iron, old fabric—that they can resell to recycling companies for $2 a day.

SMOKEY MOUNTAIN IN TONDO, MANILA

And gender plays no role for Smokey Mountain residents. Men, women, small girls and boys—they all find their way onto that heap.

"One thing that really struck me," observed Sabrina Iovino, a travel writer who visited Smokey Mountain in 2014, "was the fact that I barely saw old people. It's clear why: The average life span here is between 40 and 45. People are physically done by that age. Many others die of diseases."

And yet the strange thing was, the people I met at Smokey Mountain seemed happy to be coping with what they had. They were generous and welcoming to me. It made me think that happiness is not the same thing as satisfaction.

Why does this kind of problem persist when the economic divide is so obvious? It's not that the government is unaware of it. In the 1990s, the country's National Housing Authority kicked off a project to shut down Smokey Mountain, build low-cost public housing at the site, and provide urban resettlement sites for the country's other twenty million slum dwellers. But I saw those kids on that trash heap with my own eyes. Something isn't working.

I stayed in the Philippines for a few more weeks and churned out some easier videos—one about the country's crazy bumper-to-bumper traffic; another about the Filipinos who fought alongside the Americans in World War II; still another about the country's rich Spanish heritage. But something inside me had changed. I couldn't put my finger on it, but I felt it.

And yet when I flew out of the Philippines on Day 310, I was strangely uplifted. Despite the challenges I'd seen there—at Smokey Mountain and elsewhere—I was optimistic about the country's future. When good, kind-hearted people make up the majority of a nation's population, good things are bound to happen.

On my first day in the Philippines, I had noted that the country's popular tourism slogan was "It's More Fun in the Philippines!" That's true. But five weeks and four days later, a slightly tweaked version of the slogan kept running through my head—one that more accurately reflected what I'd felt during my stay there: "There's More Love in the Philippines."

HOW STRONG IS AN AMERICAN PASSPORT?

PUERTO RICO, DAY 704

When I was a kid, I thought that if you were a citizen of a rich and powerful country, you had certain rights, privileges, and powers, all of them granted to you by the laws and protections of your homeland.

For example, if you were a Swiss citizen stranded on top of Mount Everest and in need of urgent evacuation, your Swiss government, consulates, and embassies—along with those of Nepal—would do the impossible to get you

PUERTO RICO

off that mountain. You may be on faraway soil, but you remain a citizen of Switzerland and thus enjoy all of the protections your citizenship, and your passport, affords you.

Similarly, I was 100 percent convinced that the government of the world's most powerful country, the United States of America, would extend the same kind of help to its citizens, no matter where they were or what danger they faced.

That's what I thought until I visited Puerto Rico.

At exactly 6:15 in the morning of Wednesday, September 20, 2017, Hurricane Maria stomped onto Puerto Rican soil, carrying with her sustained winds blasting at sixty-four miles per hour—with gusts nearly twice that powerful. She touched down as a Category 4 hurricane at Yabucoa, the modest eighty-three-square-mile valley on the southeastern coast, best known for its banana plantations and hard-working inhabitants—American citizens who are nicknamed "the sugar people," because of the region's long history of sugarcane production.

By the time Maria swept off Puerto Rico at its northwestern shoreline eight hours later—its violent path having torn straight through the center of the island—it was already being regarded as the territory's worst natural

HURRICANE MARIA, SEPTEMBER 2017

disaster on record, wreaking $90 billion in damages to homes and businesses and taking nearly three thousand lives.

Yet even worse than the destruction wreaked by the storm itself was the humanitarian crisis that immediately followed: the rampant flooding, the glacially slow relief process, the deadly water shortage, the telecommunications collapse (making it impossible to call for help), and the worst electrical blackout in American history.

And all the while, suffering Puerto Ricans continued to plead for aid. It was as if the island inhabitants were shouting en masse, "We're Americans, too. Why don't you help us?"

It was against this backdrop that I decided to visit Puerto Rico with Nas Daily—six months after the hurricane struck, but with citizens still in peril. More than 150,000 continued to live without electricity, and 200,000 insurance claims had yet to be resolved.

But I was determined to be upbeat.

"This marks the end of my first day on the island of Puerto Rico!" I announced gleefully in the opening frames of my video on Day 704. "We arrived at 4:00 a.m.—spent and tired—only to be greeted by music. We checked into our hotel, which turned out to be a palace, then left to get food, which looked like a painting. We flew the drone over the island and noticed that Puerto Rico looks like a painting, too."

If my over-the-top dialogue wasn't enough of a hint as to where I was going with this, I made sure to hammer home the point with the footage I shot: stunning aerials of the El Morro citadel in San Juan harbor; quick-cut glimpses of the lavish hotel suite Alyne and I shared; colorful close-ups of the fruit and vegetables and pancakes we'd ordered for brunch; and joyful shots of my crew and me dancing to the thumping beat of calypso music—in the airport terminal, on the beach, and down the streets of this legendary island.

And in several scenes, I wore a wide-brimmed safari hat emblazoned with the Puerto Rican flag.

At first blush, Nas Daily viewers might have suspected one of two things: that I hadn't been watching the news for the previous six months, or that I was wildly insensitive in my picture-postcard depiction of a US territory that had been brought to its knees. Neither was true. I was in Puerto Rico to make a point: that no catastrophic storm—not even one as deadly as Hurricane Maria—could kill a culture.

"Puerto Rico is a Caribbean island and a US territory," I continued. "Except people here can't vote and it's not considered a state. Just six months ago, Puerto Ricans suffered from the worst natural disaster on record—many people died and homes were destroyed. But their spirit was not, and Puerto Rico is making progress. Come visit and give them some love. Trust me, every little bit helps."

It was a decision I'd made on my flight to the island. I'd read extensively about the carnage Maria had left; I'd followed the pitched battle over relief efforts; I'd heard the anguished cries for help.

And so over the next six days, I tried to provide my own kind of relief by showcasing the indestructibility of this beautiful island, and the astonishing will of its people.

I interviewed a restaurant owner named Elaine, who was hell-bent on keeping her business alive, even in the wake of this worst storm ever. Her specialty was chocolate, and with help from her Spanish chef, she featured more than forty chocolate meals on her menu—from chocolate salmon tartare, to quinoa with chocolate, to chicken and French fries marinated with chocolate. She was also quick to point out that, in the olden days, the impoverished of Puerto Rico dined on chocolate as their main meal.

I met an eighty-three-year-old widow named Jan who was looking for a husband—and, she told me, no hurricane was going to stop her search. A pianist, painter, sculptor, and horsewoman, Jan also owned a hotel—here on an island whose tourism trade had just taken a giant hit—but she was still determined to share her life with a special someone.

I even huddled on camera with the governor of Puerto Rico to talk about the commonwealth's astonishingly low tax rate—just 4 percent—and how attractive that would be to business owners and ordinary people who were considering relocating to an island paradise. I'm no tax expert or economist, I explained, but Puerto Rico could always use some enthusiastic new citizens, and the tax break seemed like another decent incentive for living there.

Yet even as I celebrated the durability of the island and its people, I was always careful to keep the hurricane and its consequences within my camera frame.

I visited with the people of a remote mountain community that was ravaged by Maria—families that were still living without electricity, rooftops, cell service, and clean water. We spoke about the irony of their American citizenship, and the fact that their passports were the envy of the world because they guarantee freedom and the American Dream. So how was it, we wondered aloud, that half a year after the storm had struck, they were still having to use car batteries, cheap water filters, and ice coolers and were living with rapidly diminishing patience?

"This is not a conservative versus liberal issue," I told Nas Daily viewers. "It's not a Republican versus Democrat issue. This is an American issue. If a country is only as strong as its most vulnerable members, then how strong is American citizenship?"

During our visit to this community, I and my two colleagues—Agon and Karam—decided to experience firsthand what these brave Puerto Ricans were being forced to endure. For one full day, we lived without electricity, clean water, or internet.

It was brutal. To make a phone call, we had to climb to the top of a mountain for a signal. (And for someone like me who's addicted to internet access, it was especially trying.) To drink, we had to draw water from the river, filter it slowly, then carefully conserve it. And in the dark of night, we had to rely on automobile batteries, loud generators, and candles in order to see.

DEPRIVATION IN THE MOUNTAINS

By the end of our first (and last) day of this, Agon, Karam, and I were genuinely frustrated. The idea that people had been living this way for six months was crazy.

And that was the whole point. To us, the tiniest problems are the end of our world. Our cable service is interrupted for a few hours; our favorite restaurant is closed; we can't hail an Uber for a whole thirty minutes—and man, how we love to complain about it (especially me).

And yet here in this stricken community in the dense forests of Puerto Rico, we saw people holding up in the face of heartbreaking adversity. Despite their tragedy, their community was strong. They appreciated nature more. They appreciated *each other* more. Right next to those loud generators, we saw families eating together happily. In the black of night, they bonded in the soft glow of candlelight.

And this kind of deprivation isn't just in post-hurricane Puerto Rico. Throughout most of the world, people struggle in ways that many in the West can't even imagine. What they live without—food, health care, education, safety—are precisely the things most of us take for granted.

During our seven days in the Caribbean, the people of Puerto Rico showed us that not even gale-force winds could extinguish the light of their candles. And as much as I tried to avoid it, I couldn't help but reframe my original question: If a country is as strong as its most vulnerable members, then how strong is an American passport?

THE AIRPORT PRISONER

195 MILES FROM MALAYSIA, DAY 877

It started with an email:

> Make a video about this guy.

I clicked on the link and was taken to the Instagram profile of a thirty-seven-year-old man. The more I read, the more alarmed I grew. Apparently, this man was living in an airport terminal in Malaysia—sleeping on the floor—with no way of getting out. He'd been stuck there for six months. His name was Hassan al-Kontar.

Hassan was from As-Suwayda, Syria, a Druze city sixty miles south of Damascus. In 2006, he immigrated to the United Arab Emirates, in part to avoid military service in his habitually war-torn homeland. He found work in the UAE as an insurance marketing manager—nice job, nice apartment, nice life—but in 2011, civil war broke out in Syria and he was summoned home to join the army. He wouldn't go.

"I didn't want to kill my people or innocent ones," he later told me. "I don't consider it right to participate in war. It's not because I am a coward or that I don't know how to fight. It's because I don't believe in war."

Although Hassan stood firmly by his pacifism ("Life is all about having a strong belief system," he explained), his troubles were just beginning. That same year his passport expired and, along with it, his work permit. He tried to have the documents renewed at the Syrian embassy in the UAE, but officials there—evidently still peeved about his refusal to join the army—rejected his applications. So Hassan went into hiding for the next six years, living underground as a man without a passport, without a job, without a country. Government authorities in the UAE eventually caught up with him in 2017 and deported him to a holding center in Malaysia, "one of the very few countries in the world which offers visas upon arrival to Syrians like me," he said. He was given a three-month tourist visa and left to his own devices.

He saved up enough money to buy a ticket to Ecuador on Turkish Airlines, but for reasons never explained to him, the airline denied him permission to board his flight and did not refund the cost of his ticket. By this point, he'd been fined by Malaysian authorities for overstaying his welcome in the country and was therefore deemed "illegal." So he tried once more to get out—this time to Cambodia—and he actually made it there. But when his flight arrived, he was refused entry into the country, had his passport confiscated, and was sent back to Kuala Lumpur. The date was March 7, 2018.

The man was now stuck. He couldn't leave Malaysia because he had no passport. He couldn't enter Malaysia because his tourist visa had expired. And if he tried to exit the airport, he'd be arrested and quite possibly sent back to Syria, where he'd surely be tossed in jail.

For the next six months, Hassan lived as a prisoner in Kuala Lumpur International Airport. He slept on a rolled-up mat under an escalator. He subsisted on surplus airline food—mostly mystery meat with rice—that was smuggled to him by sympathetic airport employees. For more than half a year, he did not leave the terminal, take a breath of fresh air, or take a warm shower—being forced, instead, to "bathe" by splashing cold water on his face in the bathroom.

He also grew mind-numbingly bored. He tended to the airport's potted plants, referring to them as "my forest." He took up crocheting. He did endless laps on the terminal's motorized walkway, calling it his "treadmill." And when some friends gave him a stuffed red dog that they'd bought at a Malaysian festival, he adopted it as a "pet," naming it Miss Crimson and taking it for walks through the terminal.

"Living in that airport was like taking the ice bucket challenge every day," he told me.

Fortunately for Hassan, his sense of humor earned him a following on social media, particularly Twitter, where he posted a regular video diary of his personal hell.

"Winter is coming," he tweeted one day, along with a photo of himself crocheting a blue scarf, "so I need to make myself ready." He also publicly volunteered to fly on a NASA expedition to Mars, concluding, "It's very clear by now that there is no place for me on this earth, as no country is allowing me in."

But not everything was funny to Hassan. In fact, his solitude was growing unbearable. During his time away from home, he had missed his brother's wedding and his father's funeral, and it was all beginning to overwhelm him.

"I'm as lonely as a sparrow in the rain," he tweeted one morning, quoting a line from *The Green Mile*, a movie about a death row inmate. "I'm tired of never having a soul to be with or a country I can call home. I'm tired of people being ugly to each other. I'm tired of all the pain I feel and hear all the time. Can you understand this, world?"

Hassan's desperate posts captured the attention of the media. Marriage proposals streamed in from women everywhere—Australia, Tahiti, the Maldives, Miami—all of which Hassan politely rejected, pointing out that arranged marriages for the purpose of citizenship were illegal. At the same time, a group of Canadians from Vancouver—complete strangers—banded together and started a crowdfunding campaign, raising the $13,600 required of Canadian citizens to privately sponsor a refugee for resettlement. They then petitioned the Canadian immigration minister—gathering tens of thousands of signatures—urging the country to take Hassan in as a legitimate refugee.

The good news was: the first phase of the Canadian application process was approved. Once in Canada, Hassan would have a new home, a new job, and a new future. The bad news? Phase two of the application process would take twenty-six months.

Hassan would have to wait in the airport for twenty-six more months.

It was amid these spiraling events that I entered the picture. In September 2018, I began getting texts from Nas Daily followers, alerting me to Hassan's plight. One of them read:

> You've got to do a video on this dude. He's stuck in the Malaysian airport and he can't leave.

At the time, I was in Singapore, a short sixty-minute flight away.

The more I thought about Hassan, the more I could relate to him. He was an Arab. He was funny. He was opposed to war and had stuck to his convictions. And, of course, he was stuck in an airport—and I hate most airports.

I decided to contact him. I found him on Instagram and sent a message:

> Hey, Hassan. It's Nas from Nas Daily. I heard about your story. Would you be interested in making a video about it?

Hassan immediately responded yes.

We connected by phone and came up with a plan. He already knew that I couldn't visit him personally—my Israeli passport isn't welcome in Malaysia—so instead I would send my colleague Agon, whose Polish passport permitted him entry into the country. The video would have to be done in one day, I told Hassan, and we'd need several hours, because it was a complicated story to tell.

Hassan agreed to the terms, and Agon jumped on a plane.

When he arrived at Kuala Lumpur International, Agon headed straight for Terminal 2, where he knew Hassan would be waiting. As planned, Hassan took Agon on a small tour of his airport prison, all the while telling his story. Just as he was on his social media posts, Hassan was candid and funny and very camera-friendly. Three hours passed in a heartbeat, and soon Agon was on a flight back to Singapore. When he arrived, I called Hassan for one more interview, then wrote the script and shot my on-camera narration, intercutting it with Agon's footage.

"Hassan's only option now is to wait twenty-six months," I said at the end of the video, "and our only option is to tell the world that this guy exists. He's living in Terminal 2 in an airport in Kuala Lumpur, behind an escalator, with no bed, no shower, no freedom, and no future. This is the story of one person who, like millions of others, is suffering because he refuses to be part of a war he doesn't believe in. It's high time he gets the attention he deserves."

We launched the video on Facebook that same night and it went superviral, clocking in eighteen million views in just a matter of days. Hassan's story had clearly struck a nerve.

In the ensuing days, we tried to stay in contact with Hassan as best we could, following his tweets and keeping tabs on the efforts to bring him to Canada. But then suddenly, Hassan's social media posts stopped. No clever tweets. No funny pictures. No pleas for relief. Just silence.

His Canadian sponsors began to panic, worrying that he'd been deported to Syria and was now sitting in a jail cell. They frantically appealed to Canada's refugee authorities, inquiring about the status of the extradition efforts and imploring them to pick up the pace. The United Nations refugee agency, meanwhile, began working with Malaysia to "get a better understanding of the circumstances."

As for those of us at Nas Daily, we cringed at the idea that whatever Hassan was going through—whether it was deportation or worse—was the result of the amped-up international exposure we'd given his story. Eighteen million views was no small thing.

One month passed. Then a second. Still no word from Hassan. The local Malaysian news reported that Hassan would be sent back to Syria. This was one of the lowest moments of my career. I had never intended to harm anyone or anything. All I did was make a video to raise awareness about this guy. But for some reason, Malaysian authorities thought the video gave Malaysia a black eye and, as a result, decided to get rid of Hassan once and for all.

But then on Monday, November 26, 2018—264 days after his ordeal had begun—Hassan posted a new video at the top of his Twitter feed.

"Hi. I know I look like someone from the Stone Ages," he said, lightly scratching at his beard, which had grown long and shaggy. "I'm sorry for that. I'm also sorry for not being in touch for the last two months. For now, it is not important where I have been or what was going on with me. What is important is the present and the future. For today, I am in Taiwan; tomorrow, I will be reaching my final destination in Vancouver, Canada.

"The last eight years was a long, hard journey," he continued, "and the last ten months was cold and hard, too. I could not have done it without the support and prayers from all of you, and without the help of my family, my new Canadian family, and my lawyer. Thank you. I love you all."

Over the next few days, Hassan would reveal the reason for his two-month disappearance. Not long after he'd appeared on Nas Daily, Malaysian authorities had arrested him for allegedly being in a restricted area of the airport without a boarding pass. He was sent to a detention center, where he was unable to communicate with the outside world. Throughout his captivity, he said, Malaysian officials repeatedly threatened him with deportation back to Syria. Fearing for his safety, Canada expedited his twenty-six-month asylum process, making him eligible for entry into the country by the end of November. International law states that an individual can't be deported if an asylum application is pending, so Malaysia had no choice in the matter. Authorities had to hand him over.

On November 26, Hassan was taken back to the airport in Kuala Lumpur and put on a plane. When he arrived in Canada, he was wearing a T-shirt, jeans, and flip-flops—and a tired but satisfied smile. He was greeted by his elated Canadian sponsors, as well as members of the press. At one point, a reporter from the Canadian Broadcast Corporation asked him how he felt to be on safe soil.

"There's a moment in life that can be more amazing and beautiful than the dream itself," Hassan answered. "I can't really describe it, but it's a feeling of love and care. And home." And then, in classic Hassan fashion, he added, "But for the time being, I need a hot shower. I've done my time in airports. No more airports. I'd rather use a horse."

At Nas Daily, we practically broke out the champagne. We immediately posted a new video, announcing the news of Hassan's release. Although the triumph was clearly a collective international effort—government agencies, lawyers, reporters, and ordinary people had joined hands to rescue this one man—I felt it was important to let my viewers know that their voices had been a crucial part of the victory.

FREE IN CANADA

"We did it—you did it!" I told them. "We made a video about a man stuck in an airport and eighteen million of you supported him—by watching and caring and acting. International pressure doesn't always follow a straight path, but you have shown that one comment, one like, one share can really make a difference. This is proof that you have power, that you can save a life, that you can change the world!"

For the first time in Nas Daily history, I felt like we'd been able to bring about real, tangible change using social media. Oftentimes, online folks like me are given a bad rap for "having no job" and "doing nothing" with our lives. Hassan's story was clear evidence that social media, used effectively, can indeed make the world a better place.

Perhaps Hassan said it best in that first video he tweeted following his release. After thanking all those around the world who had rallied on his behalf, he paused for a moment and then said softly: "And let's keep the prayer going for those who still need it the most—people in refugee and detention camps all over the world. I hope they, too, will be safe and legal as soon as possible."

POOR VS. RICH

When I was growing up, I thought everyone in the world had the same amount of money. No one was rich, no one was poor—everyone was middle class, just like my parents. As clueless as that sounds, it was kind of a sweet worldview. Maybe I was a born socialist.

But now that I'm older, I've realized that you're either rich or poor. I don't even believe in the so-called middle class anymore, because that's just a label that depends on where you live. You can make a million bucks a year in Monaco and still be considered middle class, but by international standards, you're swimming in money. It's all relative.

In the three years I spent traveling with Nas Daily, not a day went by in which I didn't see some testament to income inequality. And sometimes it was blatantly, shamefully obvious. When I traveled to India the first time, for instance, I decided to treat myself to one night in a swanky hotel. The moment I walked into my room—which looked like something out of a trendy furniture catalog—I went straight for the window to check out the view. It pulled me up short. Fifteen floors below my $200-a-night room—just beyond the hotel's chic pool-and-cabana plaza—were some of the city's poorest citizens, milling along the narrow dirt paths in their slum, which was basically an oversize, run-down parking lot crammed with fifty tin-roofed shacks.

But India was hardly the worst perpetrator of the have/have-not divide. I saw an even more striking example when I was in Brazil and got a gander at the country's notorious favelas. First cropping up in Rio de Janeiro in the nineteenth century, the favela (Portuguese for "slum") is Brazil's version of the densely populated, low-income neighborhood. In the early years favelas were urban residences occupied mainly by traveling soldiers, poor migrants, and formerly enslaved Africans. But by the twentieth century, they'd become so infested with crime and disease—and frankly were such eyesores—that government authorities began relocating favela dwellers to hundreds of shantytowns in the hills, mostly on the outskirts of barrios like Rocinha, Ipanema, and Copacabana.

I visited the Rocinha favela, which hangs on an especially steep slope overlooking Rio and is surrounded by thick tracts of trees. When I ventured inside its boundaries, I felt claustrophobic. More than seventy thousand Brazilians are squeezed into the brick and concrete homes there, and the streets are so narrow you have to use motorbikes to get around. Because there is no sewer system, favela residents store water in large tanks atop their homes, and they steal electricity—which many of them can't afford—directly from electric poles.

I was a little nervous about walking around Rocinha because crime is rampant there. I didn't use my large camera to capture images because I feared being mugged for it. Instead, I began filming on my iPhone, and in less than a minute I caught a fuzzy glimpse of a local drug lord wielding a gun.

But I did have an opportunity to launch my drone above Rocinha, and when I saw the footage, my jaw dropped. I hadn't realized just how closely the favela was situated to the rich neighborhood next door. The image spoke for itself: On the left side of the aerial view you could see the red roofs of about ten generously spaced luxury homes, their swimming pools and tennis courts clearly visible on their forested lawns. On the right side was one large, gray mass of favela rooftops—more than 150 of them—jammed so close together you couldn't see any ground separating them.

I left Rocinha convinced that Brazilian favelas aren't so much neglected neighborhoods as they are countries-stuck-within-a-country—and the only passport you need to get into them is your low income and dark skin color.

Lest we in North America think we're immune to this depressing kind of economic disparity, I saw the same sort of thing on the streets of San Francisco. I was in the city for a quick visit in November 2016, just before I took off for Japan. I was craving ice cream, so I stopped at a trendy little dessert boutique not far from City Hall. I took my place in line among the yuppies and techies, then watched the woman behind the counter whip up a small cup of vanilla for me, using a shiny silver appliance that looked like it belonged in a mad scientist's lab. Turns out that they made their ice cream with a special process that "minimizes the crystals between the ice-cream molecules, so that it's extra creamy."

I paid my $8 and walked out onto the street, already two spoonfuls into my designer ice cream, and I have to admit that it tasted extra great. But a one-minute stroll down the street from the shop, on the manicured lawn in front of City Hall, I spotted:

A homeless man with an empty suitcase taking a pee next to a park bench.

A woman wearing two overcoats lying on the sidewalk, sound asleep on top of a large sheet of cardboard.

A bag man pushing a shopping cart filled with empty soda cans.

A group of sleeping bodies, sprawled out on the grass—looking like corpses in a battlefield photo.

And all the while, well-heeled San Franciscans—not unlike those who had been waiting in line with me for the ritzy ice cream—walked right by these unfortunates as if they didn't even see them.

I might have been less annoyed if I had been in some other city, but this was San Francisco, birthplace of the iPhone and Facebook and Google. And it was disheartening to me that this top 1 percent of the city—rich people who are designing the future of the world through technology—were just a little too busy to interact with the bottom 10 percent.

So the obvious question was: What was *I* doing that was any more compassionate? Not a whole lot, to be honest. But I'd like to think that raising awareness through my videos was a good start, and one way to do that was to examine what money really buys for the rich and for the poor.

In Nairobi, Kenya, I decided to get a single haircut in two places—the right side of my head in the richest part of the city, at a spa where Barack Obama stays when he visits; and the left side in the poorest part of town, at what looked like your typical street-corner barbershop. One haircut, two Nairobis.

I did a classic split screen and filmed both barbers cutting my hair simultaneously. They used the same instruments and took the same care, both guys gently trimming around my ears and sideburns. But the settings were entirely different. The spa was lavishly appointed, and the employees wore pressed, cranberry-colored uniforms. The slum barbershop was basically a storefront joint on a littered street, where the guys who wielded the shears wore T-shirts and jeans.

Bottom line: while the cheap haircut cost $1 and the froufrou stylist charged me $10, both sides of my head looked exactly the same. So the question was, Who's getting ripped off worse here—the rich customers who are being overcharged for a routine haircut, or the poor barbers who make barely enough money to cover their rent in the poorest part of the city?

I took this little experiment one step further when I was in Mumbai a few weeks later and, like many tourists in India, had a shirt custom-made for me—only from two different shirts. First I went to an upscale mall, where I bought a slick Tommy Hilfiger number—sky-blue silk, with a delicate crosshatch pattern—and paid 3,800 rupees for it (about $55). Then I went to a small shop in a sketchy part of town—the kind where clothes are stuffed in bins—and pulled a cheap shirt off the shelf. Light black cotton, with small gray insignias on it. That one ran me 450 rupees (a little more than six bucks).

I took the shirts to a tailor and asked him to cut them both in half and then sew a rich half together with a poor half. If he thought I was nuts, he didn't let on—though he did mumble three words when he saw the price tag on the Hilfiger shirt: "Oh, my God." I watched him drag his scissors up the middle of both shirts, and I'll confess that I winced a bit when he did that, especially on the Tommy shirt. Then he meticulously sewed the two halves together, making sure that even the label inside the neck collar was similarly half-and-half.

I'm no fashion maven, but I have to say that the final product looked pretty damn sharp—though whenever I asked people to guess which side was the rich side and which was the poor side, the responses were practically even.

And that's the point. From the fancy hotel room to the favela, from the ice-cream parlor to the park bench, from the luxury hair salon to the run-down shirt shop, there are two different planets. On one of them, people have money; on the other, people don't have money—and yet the citizens of both planets are practically the same.

The reason for this thought exercise is certainly not to bash the rich. I have nothing against rich people, or poor ones. I just have three wishes: I wish to live in a world in which extreme poverty doesn't exist.

I wish to live in a world where the bottom 10 percent are pulled upward, so that they, too, can live a decent life.

And as naive as this sounds, I wish to live in a world where money didn't really matter. That way, we'd have time to focus on more important things—like each other.

IMPERFECTLY PERFECT

After a thousand days of circumnavigating the globe, I can safely say that the countries of the world fall into three categories: the developed nations, the underdeveloped nations . . . and Japan.

Japan does a lot of things wrong.

Now that I've gotten that out of the way, let me try to put into words how much Japan is doing right—and how much I love it. This is no easy task because Japan is no easy place to visit.

For one thing, Japan spent much of its history savoring its privacy. In fact, it wasn't until July 8, 1853, that the country first opened its doors to foreigners—and even that was by force. In an act of "gunboat diplomacy," Commodore Matthew Perry of the US Navy—on orders from President Millard Fillmore—steered his warships into Edo Bay, then fired off a couple of cannons to announce, "Hey, guys, we're here to trade with you!" That'll do the trick.

A century and a half later, Japan thrives as a tourism mecca, and on my Nas Daily trips to this remarkable island nation—three of them altogether—I began calling Japan "imperfectly perfect," a place where tiny hotel rooms, brutal workdays, and outrageous prices ($9 for a single grape—I kid you not) are forgiven in light of stunning mountains, impeccable order, rich culture, and crazy-smart people.

Japan is an insanely safe place to visit, and on Day 229, I put that to the test by conducting a simple experiment: I left my drone bag—with my $1,200 drone inside—on a busy sidewalk, unattended, and then went across

THE SAFE STREETS OF TOKYO

the street to film the passersby. In most other countries, people would have snatched the bag up or called the cops. But sure enough, in Tokyo, the pedestrians just walked on by. Astounded, I tried the same thing with my wallet, then with my iPhone, then with 3,000 yen—in cash. Nobody was interested. The Japanese, it turns out, have built one of the safest countries in the world.

I was equally curious to see whether the Japanese lived up to their rep as the most polite people on the planet. I had noticed when a cashier handed me back my credit card, she used both hands and surrendered a little bow of respect. I watched pedestrians on street corners regularly obey "Don't Walk" signs, even when no cars were in sight. And everyone covered their mouths when they coughed, so as not to get anyone else sick.

So I took it a step further. One afternoon I strolled around Kyoto—the former imperial capital of Japan and, arguably, one of the country's most beautiful cities—and said "arigato" (thank you) to everyone I passed, then waited to see their response. Complete strangers. No introduction.

The first person I tried it on was a teenage boy. He momentarily looked startled, then broke into a big grin, raised his hand and said "arigato" back to me. Next person, the same thing. Then the next and the next and the next. No one ignored me, no one gave me a blank or angry stare, no one walked away. They all thanked me in return for absolutely no reason. Imagine running this experiment in, say, New York. I'm guessing you'd get a few choice words in return—none of them "thank you."

And yet the one thing that I will never forget about Japan—indeed, it was one of the reasons I'd made the trip in the first place—was my visit to the city where Japan suffered the darkest day in its history: Hiroshima.

Like most travelers who flock there, I had gone to Hiroshima to do two things: learn and pay respect. Seventy-one years earlier—at 8:16 a.m. on August 6, 1945—an American World War II bomber dropped its 9,700-pound atomic payload on Hiroshima, instantly killing seventy thousand people and destroying 70 percent of the city. By the end of the year, the death toll had nearly doubled because of injuries and radiation. It was the first of only two times in history that a weapon of that magnitude was deployed on a human populace. The second time was three days later, when an equally deadly bomb was dropped on Nagasaki, killing eighty-seven thousand more.

"I'm not going to pretend I know how to describe this tragic event," I told viewers from a bridge overlooking the Motoyasu River. "That's because I can't. So I'm just going to leave it to the visuals."

And that's what I did—capturing quiet portraits of Hiroshima as I saw it that day, beneath a blanket of fog and drizzle.

Japanese businessmen, heading to work beneath their black umbrellas.

A lone ferry, cutting across Hiroshima Bay.

And the striking red-orange *torii*—or floating gate—that lingers in the waters off nearby Itsukushima Island.

Most important, I sent up my drone so that viewers could see the city just as the crew of the B-29 bomber saw it on that warm Monday morning seven decades ago.

When I edited the segment that evening, I subtitled it with a running quotation from a speech President Barack Obama had given when he'd visited Hiroshima seven months earlier: "We have known the agony of war. Let us now find the courage, together, to spread peace and pursue a world without nuclear weapons."

I will never forget looking at the final video and breaking down in tears. That day was one of the loneliest, most solemn of my journey. No matter how many years pass, Hiroshima is still Hiroshima. For me, it certainly wasn't easy to spend the day walking on such sacred ground—beneath the clouds, in the rain—with no one there to share the sadness with. It remains for me a profoundly moving memory.

I stayed in Hiroshima for an additional day, searching for a symbol of hope in a city that was punished worse than any other in history.

That symbol, it turned out, was on the very same spot

HIROSHIMA PEACE MEMORIAL PARK

TORII, HIROSHIMA BAY

where I'd made my first video. Draped across the narrow strip of land where the Motoyasu and Ota rivers meet is a beautiful, thirty-acre park that honors the memory of Hiroshima—with monuments, sculptures, exhibition halls, a museum, and, just across the river, the skeletal remains of the Genbaku Dome, the only building left standing in the vicinity of the bomb blast. In keeping with the spirit of the Japanese people, this gentle plot of land is not called a war memorial but a peace memorial.

I come from a place on earth where the conflict is almost as old as the Hiroshima bombing, and the fighting there still persists. Other countries just won't let it go. But in Hiroshima, the Japanese—young and old, men and women—have rebuilt their faith in humanity alongside their magnificent skyscrapers and bullet trains.

As one survivor told me, "The spirit of Hiroshima is to endure grief, transcend hatred, pursue harmony and prosperity, and yearn for genuine, lasting world peace. Because peace never flows from hate."

NAS STORIES
SRI LANKA **THE KEYBOARD WARRIOR**

The term *keyboard warrior* is typically used as a social media diss, but in the case of Irfan Hafiz, it was a noble and most fitting title. Born in the coastal city of Matara in Sri Lanka, Irfan was stricken at age four with Duchenne muscular dystrophy, a rare and severe muscle disease that landed him in a wheelchair at age twelve, then flat on his stomach in bed at age eighteen. And for the next nineteen years, Irfan stayed in that bed, fully conscious but unable to move. Doctors hadn't given him long to live, but Irfan had other ideas. Driven by frustration, boredom, and anger—and despite a collapsed muscle system that left him strength in only a single finger—Irfan began to write. And write. And write. One letter at a time. When he couldn't type on a laptop, he typed on an iPhone, all the while connected to a ventilator that sat at his bedside. By the time I met Irfan, he was thirty-seven and had already published three books that had sold in the thousands—*Silent Struggle*, a memoir written as poetry; *Moments of Merriment*, a young adult novel; and *Silent Thoughts*, a deeply personal collection of life lessons. Nas Daily followers fell in love with Irfan, viewing his video twenty million times and sharing it just as widely. Irfan was energized by this outpouring of support and dove even more passionately into his fourth book. "I feel like I have a new life," he told me. Tragically, that rebirth was short-lived: Irfan died just two months after I met him. And yet, even in death, Irfan inspired me more than any other person I've met, teaching me not only how to live life, but how to fight for it every day. "The greatest battle," he wrote in *Silent Thoughts*, "takes place nowhere else but within ourselves." If that's the case, Irfan, you won your battle. Rest in peace, brother.

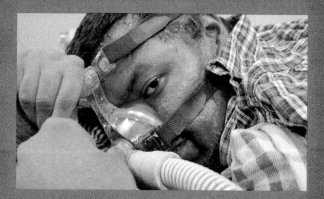

ISRAEL HELP IS ON THE WAY!

By the time you finish reading this page, someone's life may have been saved. For that we can thank Eli Beer, the forty-six-year-old founder of United Hatzalah of Israel, a nonprofit, all-volunteer emergency medical service that specializes in speed. As a young EMT in Jerusalem, Eli couldn't help but notice how the congested streets of the city brought conventional ambulances to a standstill, often making the difference between someone surviving or dying from a heart attack or other traumatic event. So in 2002, Eli developed a fleet of rapid-response "ambucycles"— medically retrofitted motorbikes that can easily squeeze and weave through bumper-to-bumper traffic and deliver life-saving help to victims before the big ambulance arrives. To ride those bikes, Eli recruited everyday volunteers—schoolteachers, engineers, waitresses—and put them through six months of rigorous EMT training before issuing each one an ambucycle and medical equipment. Finally, Eli built a command center, also staffed by volunteers, and that's where the action begins: an emergency call comes in, a dispatcher locates the nearest ambucycler through GPS tracking, and help arrives at the victim's side within three minutes, sometimes in ninety seconds. "Think of it like Uber," Eli told me proudly, "only we don't charge for our service and we save lives!" To date, United Hatzalah's all-volunteer army of guardian angels—five thousand Jews, Muslims, and Christians working side by side—have treated 3.5 million people in more than twenty countries. It's an organization that is 100 percent cost-free—and, adds Eli, "100 percent human."

THE UNITED STATES
THE CRAZY LIFE OF BEN

I traveled the world to meet people, but as it turns out, one of the most interesting was in my own backyard. I've known Ben Yu since 2011, when we met on Facebook. He's four days older than me and he defines the word *unique*. Here's a quick sampling of his crazy life: He got into Harvard, became depressed, dropped out after one semester, traveled to all seven continents in one year, and bought an RV—with a bed, bathroom, and kitchen—in San Francisco and lived in it for three years, saving $50,000, which he used to buy an island in Canada. Still with me? Moving

on. By his own account "impulsive," he got married to a woman after two dates, got divorced, and got $100,000 from a billionaire to start a company that failed, but kept inventing things, including two body sprays (one to give you more energy, the other to make you sleepy). He drives a Mini, has three tattoos ("they represent the three women in my life who have scarred me"), donates his bone marrow every ten weeks, and for a while would eat only canned food that was made that year—or forty years ago for soldiers in Vietnam. In January 2018, Ben became

a millionaire from a $15,000 investment in Bitcoin and immediately began sharing the wealth, including buying a van for a friend to live in next to his RV and handing $5 to every homeless person he saw on the street. Ben was a Nas Daily favorite— the only person to have been featured in five separate videos, each one drawing more than one million views. But most important, Ben is one of the kindest, smartest, strangest, coolest, and most generous people I have ever met.

HONG KONG THE WORLD'S BEST METRO

I always considered transportation a pretty boring topic—all I really cared about was getting where I needed to go. But then I took a spin on the Hong Kong Metro and everything changed. Hands down, it is the best subway system on the planet. Composed of 136 miles of rail and 59 sparkling stations (so clean you can sleep on the floor!), Hong Kong's Mass Transit Railway (MTR) boasts an on-time rate of 99.9 percent. Why so punctual? Because system operators are charged a fine of HK$1 million any time a train runs more than thirty minutes late. And the good stuff doesn't end there. The cars are air-conditioned, there's free Wi-Fi, glass safety doors separate the tracks from the trains (picture your typical airport shuttle), and uniformed station attendants are always standing by to lend a helping hand. And all of this will cost you just 70 cents, which beats the hell out of the highway robbery on the New York and London subways. Oh, and did I mention that the MTR provides all of this and still manages to turn a profit? How often can you say that about a government agency? I know I sound smitten, but don't just take my word for it—Hong Kong's MTR moves five million commuters every single day.

SENEGAL THE ISLAND OF PEACE

Some beachside cities like to call themselves a haven for seashell collectors, but the residents of Joal-Fadiouth on Senegal's Petite Côte can go one better: their whole damn island is made completely of clamshells. I'm not kidding—the homes, the buildings, even the floors bear a seashell motif I've never seen anywhere else in the world. As its hyphenated name implies, Joal-Fadiouth is actually two townships in one: Joal is the fishing village on the mainland, and Fadiouth is the seashell isle, which connects to the shore by a wooden footbridge. But as photogenic as the top-to-bottom clamshell decor may be, what wowed me even more was what I witnessed among its people: eight thousand Muslims and Christians existing in complete harmony. They pray together in their churches and mosques; they relax with one another beneath giant eight-hundred-year-old baobab trees; and they bury their dead next to each other in a cemetery that's also built from shells. And there's not a motorized vehicle in sight. No one's quite sure of how Joal-

Fadiouth came into being—competing theories trace its original settlers to places as far-flung as Gambia and Morocco. But it hardly makes a difference because, for the past one hundred years, its calling card has been its inhabitants' peaceful coexistence. We often look to First World countries to understand the melting pot of humanity, but I have yet to see a more perfect example of unity than on this tiny developing island made from shells.

PART 3
FUN & ADVENTURE

OH, MY MALTA!

Oh! My! Malta!

I swear, I barely remember saying it.

We'd just arrived in Malta, the tiny island nation that floats serenely in the Ionian Sea about seventy miles south of Sicily's southern shore. We were unpacking our gear when I looked out the window and suddenly got my first real glimpse of the surrounding beauty. I had intended to say "Oh, my God!" but inadvertently, it came out of my mouth ridiculously wrong:

"Oh, my Malta!"

What I didn't know then, but would quickly discover, was that those three words—an enthusiastic expression of both surprise and delight—would perfectly capture the magic Malta had in store for me.

I'd touched down at the airport knowing only that this little dot on the Mediterranean map was densely populated and, like many beach resort islands, formerly a British colony. I assumed, then, that the country's culture would be predictable and that my week there would be a nice but forgettable stopover between my more serious visits to Senegal and Australia.

Boy, was I wrong.

The entire country is a living superlative: its capital, Valletta, is the smallest in Europe; its churches are the largest in Christianity; and its exuberant citizens express *ferh* (Maltese for "joy") in the strangest and most charming of ways.

Case in point: When a seafaring tanker ran aground in Malta just a few months before our arrival, the country mourned the disaster for about forty

THE MALTA SHIPWRECK, AN INSTAGRAM FAVORITE

seconds—then turned a dramatic photo of the lopsided shipwreck into an Instagram sensation.

Maybe I became a little obsessed, but my instant crush on this offbeat, intoxicating country led me to conclude that "Oh, my Malta!" was too fitting a catchphrase to go to waste. So starting the next day, Nas Daily went on an all-out campaign to turn that snappy slogan into the country's tourism tagline.

We gathered throngs of students across the island—on streets, on beaches, in parks—to chant "Oh, my Malta!" on camera, en masse.

We dropped by Malta's Ministry for Tourism and got the staff there to add their voices to the growing "OMM!" chorus.

We even paid a visit to the president of Malta herself—Marie-Louise Coleiro Preca—who not only treated Nas Daily viewers to her own rendition of "Oh, my Malta!" but even threw in a little ad-lib at the end, saying, "Thank you so much, young people."

And, of course, we gave our new obsession a hashtag: #OhMyMalta!

As a capstone to our efforts, I threw a huge bash in Valletta, inviting the entire nation to come together under the banner of peace, love, and "Oh, my Malta!" And come they did. The impromptu celebration not only drew more than forty-three hundred people—1 percent of the country's population—but many from outside of Malta as well. For me, this was the greatest reward of all—a confirmation that unity and positivity are alive and well on the planet, even on this most unpretentious of islands.

Now, if I were a dishonest guy, I'd end the story right here, letting you believe that my "Oh, my Malta!" scheme went off flawlessly—on point, on time, and without a hitch. But I'm not dishonest, and there *were* problems.

Amid the buildup to the big party, Seb Tanti Burlo, a popular political cartoonist for the nation's leading newspaper, used "Oh, my Malta!" in one of his drawings as an ironic commentary on Malta's tourism industry after a double-decker tour bus had crashed into a tree, killing two and injuring fifty. Burlo was crucified in the local media for his shocking and intentionally tasteless cartoon, but he stuck to his guns. "This scribble I did is disgusting," he said. "It is offensive and it should offend you—because this situation is offensive. Be angry at the situation, not at me." I was interviewed about it, and I publicly supported Burlo for using his artistry—and my slogan—in an effort to address pressing issues and provoke conversation.

Next, I was accused in the media of being paid on the sly by the Maltese government for the videos I was making; for using Maltese churches, people, and even the president as "props" to advance my own interests; and for "ignoring" issues that were important to the country. Broadsided and pissed off, I set the record straight in interviews and Facebook posts, not only denying the fictional charges but also revealing that I actually stood a chance of losing money on the party. To its credit, the Maltese media printed my rebuttals in full.

MOSTA, MALTA: THE BASILICA OF THE ASSUMPTION OF OUR LADY

Finally came the most infuriating—but, in retrospect, unsurprising—affront of all. In the run-up to its upcoming mass meeting, the country's Labour Party appropriated my Nas Daily logo, as well as my "Oh, my Malta!" slogan, to create T-shirts that promoted its agenda. That was a Maltese bridge too far.

"I don't like this," I barked on Facebook. "No one party can claim this slogan, and certainly no party can claim Nas Daily. I have no idea what each party stands for, but I have a strong desire not to be associated with either. 'Oh, my Malta!' is not mine to dominate. It belongs to everybody."

The dustup earned me a lot of support from the Maltese people ("It takes an outsider to see just how messed up we are," one local posted on Facebook),

but one reporter called me naive for thinking so highly of Malta in the first place, so I took the gloves off.

"Brother, I am Palestinian-Israeli," I responded to the critic. "I know a thing or two about war, politics, assassinations, marginalization. It was my reality for eighteen years. But I still deeply believe that divisions can be healed in Malta. I'm not naive or optimistic. I just genuinely feel that all division is temporary. In the long run, we are one."

Despite the petty politics we experienced there, my Malta experience still tops the "win" column. Indeed, nine months later, when it came time to select the one place on the planet where I wanted to wrap up my thousand-day journey, I didn't think twice. The choice was a no-brainer:

Oh, my Malta.

STRANGERS MAKE
THE BEST FRIENDS

"Be careful of strangers."

That's what my mom always told me. And like the good boy I was trying to be, I grew up thinking that, indeed, I should be cautious around people I didn't know.

Until I found myself surrounded by forty strangers.

It was Day 272, and I'd just landed in the Philippines. As with every other country I'd traveled to, I knew relatively little about where I was and who was there. I had exactly one friend in the Philippines—someone I'd known in college—and that was it. So I decided to take a bold new step in my Nas Daily journey by hosting a "meetup" for the strangers who followed me on Facebook.

"Let's meet at 4:00 p.m. at the Starbucks Plaza this coming Sunday," I posted on my Nas Daily page, being careful to make the post visible only to followers from the Philippines. I included a generic picture of myself above the post and crossed my fingers.

Two days later, I strolled into an empty Starbucks Plaza, sat on a generic Starbucks bench, and waited.

It was my first attempt at meeting, in person, any of the enthusiastic viewers who had been following my journey to date. At once, I had two fears: (1) that no one was going to show up, and (2) that if they did show up, there would be serious awkwardness. These were people I didn't know. What would we talk about? Even worse, what if they had ulterior motives and wanted to harm me? Maybe Mom was right about strangers.

Four o'clock arrived and no one was there.

I sat on the bench sipping my coffee, pretending it was not a big deal. But it *was* a big deal. I was spiraling, wondering why I had thought anyone would come in the first place, doubting my platform and my connectedness and my value, and then suddenly, I felt someone staring at me. I looked up, and sure enough, a young man was looking at me with that kind of expression that said he recognized me from somewhere. I glanced to his left and saw another young man staring. Then a woman. Then two more. Slowly but surely, these strangers began multiplying and drifting in my direction. Ten of them. Then twenty. Thirty. Forty.

By 5:00 p.m., I found myself surrounded by forty strangers, all of whom had come from around Manila just to say hello to me. Some had driven for hours, they told me. And so, of course, my second fear never materialized. There was no awkwardness. There was no danger. For the next two hours, I basked in the friendship of forty strangers, each one friendlier than the next. We made a video together. We took pictures. We laughed. And not a single thing went wrong—which was the biggest surprise of all, because even in the best of circumstances, something always goes wrong.

MEETUP IN MALTA

Not this time. It was the most exhilarating thing I had ever done. I had taken my mother's warning to "be careful of strangers" and flipped it on its head. From that day forward, "be excited by strangers" was my new life mantra, and I took it around the world with me.

In the weeks and months that followed that first successful gathering in the Philippines, I made meetups a regular part of my Nas Daily itinerary in more than thirty countries. I would choose a popular location—centrally located, public, easy to get to—then announce it shortly after my arrival. Sometimes the turnout wasn't so hot; in Myanmar, I counted twelve heads, total. Other times, the reception was beyond my wildest dreams—like in Malta, where more than forty-three hundred people showed up. *Complete strangers.*

And I always made my events free. The way I figured it, these people were doing me a favor simply by showing up. Why on earth would I charge someone to be my friend?

And that, I think, is what made the meetups so special. They quickly became my *happy spot.* A place to connect. A moment to embrace the spirit of a country and its people. And on a much more personal level, the meetups were a kind of reward for me. What most Nas Daily followers never saw— even those who watched every day—was all the tedious and hard work that went on behind the scenes. Booking flights and hotel rooms. Scouting locations. Repairing equipment. Paying bills. So in a very real sense, the meetups became my special moment to let go of that tension and worry and take a few hours to enjoy what all that planning had produced.

A reporter once asked me about my meetups. "They always look so joyful," he said to me. "How is it that you're so comfortable around people you don't even know?"

"That's the whole point," I responded. "I'm around people I'm *about to know,* and that's what makes it so special. I love getting to know strangers."

Of all the Nas Daily meetups we did, however, the most memorable—and arguably the wildest—was the time I invited the entire country of Israel for a get-together. But this time, the location was not a Starbucks or some fountain at the center of town. This time it was as personal as it gets: my parents' house in Arraba.

I was back home, wrapping up my first year of Nas Daily, when I decided to put to rest once and for all the two greatest myths about Arab cities: (1) that they're dangerous, and (2) that Jews aren't allowed in. So I announced on Facebook that I was throwing a big meetup at my home that Saturday and that everyone was invited ("as long as you're not a murderer," I added).

Because there are no street addresses in Arraba, I posted the GPS coordinates to my house, on-screen, adding, "If you get lost, just ask for the home of Ziad Yassin, the psychologist." That's my father.

"This is not some *kumbaya-namaste* meeting or a business networking event," I told my viewers. "It's just a gathering of friends from different walks of life."

I'll admit I was a little nervous. I had no idea how many people would show up—could be three, could be three thousand—and I'm not exactly Martha Stewart when it comes to party-planning. "We will have snacks and stuff... I think," I wrote on Facebook, knowing full well that the job of refreshments would fall to my mom and sister, that my father would be in charge of gathering chairs and supplies, and that my kid brother would do  the vacuuming before guests arrived. My job was to pace back and forth.

As it turns out, there was no need for worry. About seventy-five people showed up—just enough for a comfortably packed house, but not too many to be overwhelming. More important, the final list of attendees lived up to everything I'd dreamed it would be: a gathering in which the Muslim, the Jew, and the Christian; the Indian and the American; the German and Japanese; the singles, the couples, and the disabled, were all under one roof, having fun and making friends.

I was elated. In fact, I was so happy with how the night turned out that I tried it again just three months later. It was the month of Ramadan, so this time I made it a theme party, inviting the world to join my family as we celebrated the last day of fasting and welcomed the first day of Eid—the three-day festival in which Muslims express their thanks to Allah for helping them get through their monthlong fast.

But there was one complication. In the ninety days since the first party, Nas Daily's audience had grown from 500,000 to 1.5 million. The math alone told me to expect at least 225 people this time—and the RSVPs were quickly confirming that: 300 followers had already accepted my invitation, and another 900 had expressed interest.

"It's turning out to be a bit more than I thought it would be," I sheepishly told my parents. "Don't worry—I'll cancel it."

And that's when my parents reminded me why I am, perhaps, the luckiest son on earth.

"No, wait," they said. "We can do this!"

So the planning began. Instead of borrowing some extra chairs, we got three hundred. Instead of buying one basket of fruit, we ordered many. And instead of cooking a few dozen hot meals, we decided to go the buffet route, planning a menu that would feed a tribe.

We flew my older brother in from Germany to lend a hand. We leveled the grass on our front lawn, turning it into a parking lot. Then my mom told me to go get a haircut. "You'll look nicer on camera," she said.

The day before the party, I posted a reminder. "Don't come just for food or to meet me," I cautioned. "Come to make new friends."

And you know what? That's exactly what they did. Nine busy days after sending out that first invitation, I was standing in my yard, surrounded by three hundred people who'd come from around the world—Spain, Hong Kong, the United States—just to celebrate the end of Ramadan with my family in our home.

As I've often said, I never get tired of learning, and what this one amazing evening taught me is that magic sometimes happens. Even in our troubled world, you can actually share your home address with 1.5 million strangers

PARTY PREP

on the internet, and new friendships will bloom as each new guest arrives. The traveling family, the retired couple, the pregnant tourist, the funny juggler, the guy on the motorcycle, the girl with the rainbow-colored hair. They will all come to share in your life and, in return, share a little part of theirs.

Was there a 1 percent chance that one of my guests could have been a bad person bent on doing bad things? Yes, of course—bad things happen every day. But who would want to miss the 100 percent certainty that something wonderful would happen in a house full of strangers?

WHY I DON'T BUY THINGS

Two years. *Two years.* That's how long I've been living out of a suitcase. And inside that suitcase, here is what I carry:

Ten T-shirts, some underwear, and one pair of pants.

This is not the way I've always been. Before Nas Daily, I had a lot of things in my home, and I liked to surround myself with them.

My computer. My video games. My books.

But now I own very little—and I buy almost nothing. Over the past two years, I've been in some of the greatest shopping malls in the world, but when I walk through their shops, I spend zero dollars. This isn't because I'm cheap. It's because anything that I'm considering buying has to pass what I call "The Mountain Test."

The rules for The Mountain Test are quite simple. If the item I'm thinking about buying is worth carrying up a mountain—on my back, with no hassle—then I'll buy it. If it's not, then I'll put it back on the shelf. Why? Because if I bought everything that I liked, it would be impossible to climb the mountain more than ten feet.

I know this from experience. On Day 48, I was in the Himalayas in Nepal, and I hired two guides to accompany me as I trekked the legendary Annapurna Massif. Climbing a mountain can get pretty boring; so at one point, I asked the guides to let me try carrying the backpacks they'd been lugging up the mountain. I barely made it fifteen steps.

"You think your job is hard?" I asked my viewers. "Try carrying this crap for hours on end . . . in the mountains of Nepal . . . for $10 a day!"

The Mountain Test is an extreme example, I realize, but the idea behind it is worth thinking about. Every day, we carry a lot of stuff inside us. Our worries about our jobs. Our relationships with our friends and families. Our responsibilities and our dreams. And though we think we can carry all that heavy stuff, it eventually begins to weigh us down—and when that happens, we become paralyzed, unable to move forward.

I'm not suggesting you forget your troubles and let it all go. Just like all that cool stuff on the store shelves, the things that matter to us will always be there. But we shouldn't feel like we have to burden ourselves with trying to carry so much at one time. That can get difficult, because life is a pretty steep climb.

As for my Mountain Test, I still stand by it. There are a lot of things we don't need to have on the top of a mountain, or inside a house, or anywhere in our lives, really. And I remain convinced that, traveling or not, the fewer weighty things we have to carry, the closer we will be to reaching the peak of freedom.

HOW I ENTERED A COUNTRY I'M BANNED FROM

PAKISTAN (SORT OF), DAY 449

I feel sorry for my friend Zeina. For her, seeing the world is a headache. Even though she's lived in Jordan for eighteen years, Zeina is an Iraqi citizen; and because her homeland isn't on the friendliest of terms with many other nations, her Iraqi passport is the second weakest in the world (after Afghanistan), permitting her to travel to only thirty-two countries without a visa. Compare that to a place like Germany, whose golden passport permits its citizens visa-free access to 166 countries, and you'll see why, for Zeina, traveling the globe is one giant visa nightmare.

My situation is considerably better. As an Israeli citizen with an Israeli passport, I'm permitted visa-free travel to 146 countries. And yet because of that very same passport, there are certain places I *can't* go. Some of those are Algeria, Bangladesh, Brunei, Iran, Iraq, Kuwait, Lebanon, Libya, Oman, Pakistan, Saudi Arabia, Sudan, Syria, United Arab Emirates, and Yemen.

That means that, no matter how hard I try, I can't obtain visas to visit those countries because no such visas exist. Bottom line: because of my Israeli passport, I'm banned from visiting the majority of the Arab world—which is sort of ironic because I'm an Arab myself. Israel, as it so happens, is 20 percent Arab.

But that's politics for you.

So whenever anyone says to me, "Hey, Nas, show us Algeria!" or "We'd love to see Lebanon!" I usually respond, "I wish I could, but they simply won't let me in."

But in May 2017, I had a different solution to this dilemma. I was in Istanbul, Turkey, when I started getting the strangest text messages from Pakistan.

> Nas, visit our country next!
> Nas, we love you in Pakistan. Let us show you around!
> Yo, man, come on over—you're practically next door!

Forgetting for a moment that Pakistan is as "next door" to Istanbul as Miami is to Sacramento, I was intrigued by the idea—because, from what I'd read, Pakistan is an amazing country. Birthplace to some of the oldest civilizations on earth, it's also a living picture postcard, teeming with rivers and valleys, forests and glaciers, and five of the sickest mountains on the planet—including the notorious K2.

But it was the people of Pakistan I was most interested in getting to know. Throughout the run of Nas Daily, the only way I could interact with Pakistanis was online, but even then I could tell that they were among the warmest and most welcoming of my followers. They seemed proud of their country, their heritage, and their hospitality; and they were tired of the negative press about their homeland. Indeed, while the 2011 capture and killing of Osama bin Laden inside Pakistan was heralded as a red-letter day for the United States, it only served to damage Pakistan's international image, painting the country as little more than a creepy desert hideout for global terrorists.

And yet as much as I longed to see Pakistan up-close and personal, I simply couldn't.

So I had an idea.

"I've received a ton of messages asking me to come to Pakistan," I announced on Day 404, "and it hurts to say no every time. But as you know, my Israeli passport forbids me to visit, even though I'm Muslim. So no matter how many times you invite me to Pakistan, I have to turn you down. What I

LIFE IN PAKISTAN

can do, however, is make a video about Pakistan without being there—but I need your help."

My idea was sweet, simple, and even a little cute: I would have Pakistanis write and shoot my Nas Daily video for me. They would go into their local streets with their cameras and cell phones and capture the sights and scenes I wasn't allowed to see in person. And to make it more real, I asked them to print out a picture of my face so that we could pretend I was there with them. Once they'd shot footage, I explained, they would send it to me, and I'd edit it together and upload it to Nas Daily.

This was more than just a stunt—it was a statement. It would show how a Palestinian-Israeli guy who is banned from entering a country could still make a video with the help of locals who, according to some, were supposed to hate him. My following clearly caught the spirit of this crazy project, because, almost immediately, messages from Pakistanis began piling up in my in-box. In fact, to get things rolling, I announced a physical meetup in Lahore, Pakistan, for a few days later—without me there, of course—and to my delight, thirty-five people showed up just to make a video on my behalf. That's nuts.

Over the next forty-five days, I went back to the business of Nas Daily, visiting four countries—Madagascar, New Zealand, the United States, and Israel—and throughout that entire time, my Pakistani home team was hard at work collecting footage. The more video clips they sent me, the more excited I grew. It was like we were putting together this big, global arts-and-crafts project. *I'm gonna get in trouble for this somehow,* I mused to myself at one point, *but I'll take the risk.*

By Day 449, all of the footage had come in. I took a day to assemble it, slap on the titles, and bring in the music and narration. Then I crossed my fingers and threw the video up on Facebook.

It was basic—but incredible.

The video opened with the footage from the meetup, with nearly three dozen Pakistanis standing in what appeared to be a city park and waving at the camera. "Welcome to Pakistan!" they shouted in unison.

At the front of the group, a young woman wearing a pink and red *salwar kameez* (a traditional thigh-length shirt) held a picture of my head, which she rocked back and forth in sync to the narration I'd overdubbed: "What you see behind me is a group of friends who got together to help me make a video about their country, Pakistan," my disembodied head said. "Because of my passport—and their passports—we are not allowed to visit each other. But thanks to the internet, I can show you Pakistan and see it for myself— through them."

And then I began to roll the footage that my new Pakistani friends had shot, a lively collage of clips showing Pakistanis going about their daily lives— from a fellow steering his horse up a rocky mountain slope, to children and adults playing cricket (a national obsession), to a vendor in an open market selling lingerie to women wearing Muslim garb.

"THAT'S ONE MINUTE, SEE YOU TOMORROW!"

"I needed to meet these people," I said in the video's final seconds, "but I didn't need to visit Pakistan to discover that they are some of the most welcoming in the world."

And with that, all of us—my new friends in Pakistan and me in Israel, two thousand miles away—shouted together, "That's one minute, see you tomorrow!"

The response to the video was everything I'd hoped for.

"Even though I'm Indian," one follower posted, "I've met many Pakistanis and I know how amazing they are. They are just like us. There's not much cultural difference between us—just different borders."

"Even if the government doesn't let you in the country," wrote another, "the Pakistan people will always let you into their hearts."

"I love Pakistan," wrote a third. "Damn all those passports for labeling people and restricting access. The world belongs to everyone."

I was deeply moved.

In terms of production value, was the video any good? Not really—it was low-grade Android footage.

In terms of plot, was it compelling? No again. The story arc was pretty simple. "I saw this" and "I saw that."

But in terms of what the video said—and the feelings it had elicited on my Facebook page—I was prouder of that video than any I'd done to date.

Since the dawn of time, humanity has struggled with itself—building borders, manufacturing wars, and finding countless ways to keep us separate from each other, including something as simple as a piece of paper that tells us where we can go and who we can meet. And in just sixty seconds, a small band of strangers proved that no matter the politics, humans are humans everywhere.

Welcome to Pakistan.

If there's one thing I like more than saving money, it's making money, and in Arequipa, Peru, I found a fourteen-year-old kid who's already got that whole thing figured out. José Adolfo Quisocala Condori was just twelve when he noticed that his classmates were spending their allowances at the mall but never managing to save anything. So he came up with a solution that made perfect sense: he started a bank. José collected his classmates' money and deposited the cash into individual savings accounts, issuing each of his new clients a debit card that capped their spending. "It's the first bank in the world started by a kid," José told me with a boyish smile. But that was only the beginning. He also built a system that helps kids make—and save—

money by recycling plastic. Whether it's an empty juice bottle at the bottom of their backpacks or plastic waste they find on the street, José's customers redeem these recyclables at the bank for real centimos that go straight into their accounts. The idea caught fire, and today José's Banco Cooperativo del Estudiante boasts three thousand accounts, $50,000 in savings, and eight employees who are twice his age. And not only that, in 2018, the Swedish energy company Telge Energi awarded José and his eco-bank its international Children's Climate Prize for teaching kids about saving their money and saving the environment. "It's a win-win!" says José.

MALTA HE HAS HIS OWN ISLAND

They say no man is an island, but I know a guy who comes pretty close. Salvu Vella, sixty-seven, lives on Comino, a tiny island in the Maltese archipelago. His family's presence on Comino dates back one hundred years—at one time there were seventeen of them, working jobs that no longer exist. But now the clan has dwindled to just Salvu and two cousins, and with the exception of the occasional beach-slumming tourist, they've got the whole place to themselves. Given his solitude, you'd think Salvu would be the loneliest man on earth, but when I visited for a day, he was not only joyful, but crazy busy. Dressed in head-to-toe hunter's camouflage, he took me on a whirlwind tour of his private paradise, which you can cross by foot in less than an hour. As the island's official eco-conscious custodian—a gig that earned him a National Order of Merit from Malta's president herself—Salvu has built or invented a practical showroom of vehicles and contraptions, including a motorized boat trailer, a solar-powered water-purification system, chemical-free pest control for his fields, and a fully electric all-terrain vehicle. When he's not busy fishing, farming, beekeeping, or building something, Salvu can be found at his desk browsing the web ("My internet is faster than yours!" he boasted) or outside flying one of his eleven drones. But his heart—and humanity—remains with his family. In 2011, his brother Angelo suffered kidney failure, so now Salvu is his caretaker, transporting him to the hospital for treatment every two days. Does this interfere with Salvu's round-the-clock island maintenance? "No, no," he told me. "Family always comes first."

THE UNITED STATES
HE SHOT FOR THE SKY

Just like in the song, he came straight outta Compton—only in his case, the fame happened when he came *back* to it. On July 16, 2016, Isaiah Cooper, age sixteen, made history by becoming the youngest African American ever to pilot a plane around the contiguous United States—an eight-thousand-mile journey that had begun at Compton/Woodley Airport in Southern California, then soared on to Maine, Washington, and Florida before returning back to Compton. No small

feat by any measure, Isaiah's continental cloud-hopping was especially impressive given his age (still too young to rent a car!) and the hood he'd grown up in. Compton is famous for producing some pretty tough characters—rappers and gang members among them—and, indeed, Isaiah briefly fell in with a sketchy crowd during his early adolescence. Lucky for him, though, his mom enrolled him in an aviation academy right across the street, one that was specifically geared toward inner-city, at-risk youth. Under the mentorship of Robin Petgrave—the founder of the aviation school and a Hollywood stunt helicopter pilot—Isaiah not only earned his wings but watched his grade point average also take flight, from 2.0 to 3.5. I first met Isaiah when Nas Daily was in Los Angeles, one year after his legendary journey, and he was already mulling a follow-up challenge of flying around the globe. But for my money, this determined young man's triumph was more than just an exercise in breaking records and breaking stereotypes. It was actually an awesome demonstration of the power of the human spirit, and proof positive that no heights are impossible to reach.

ECUADOR WHERE EGGS DON'T FALL?

The earth's equator passes through eleven countries, but no one celebrates pride in that cool distinction better than the people of Quito, Ecuador, where my team and I spent the day reveling in all things equatorial. As we all know, the equator (which gives Ecuador its name) is the invisible beltline that separates the earth's Northern and Southern Hemispheres, right at the waist; and in Quito, that line is painted onto the ground in bright yellow. People from around the world take selfies straddling that line—one foot in the north, the other in the south—but it's the science part that jazzed me the most. Because you're standing dead center on the earth's curve, water draining from a sink doesn't swirl left or right as it exits the basin—it goes straight down. Similarly, it is said that you can balance an egg on the head of a nail at the equator, and it doesn't fall off (a cute party trick that doesn't always work). Also, because of the equator's relationship to the sun, twice a year your shadow disappears at high noon. Unfortunately, a few purist-tourists in our group were checking the GPS on their phones and pointing out that some of the attractions in Quito—such as the sundial at the Ciudad Mitad del Mundo—were a few degrees off (there's a party pooper in every crowd). But I didn't care about any of that. I was just happy to see people getting excited about the planet they live on.

SENEGAL THE ONE-THOUSAND-PERSON GYM

By Day 712 of my journey, I had a pretty good way of determining my interest in a country: if what I was seeing was predictable, I wasn't so enthralled; but if what I was seeing was surprising, it had my undivided attention. The nation of Senegal was the very definition of unpredictability—and I learned that within hours of my arrival. I'd wandered onto the sprawling Fann Beach in the capital city of Dakar to give my drone a spin above the shoreline when I suddenly noticed crowds of people working out together, right there on the sand. At first I thought I'd stumbled onto a soccer or basketball team warming up before a big game, but I quickly learned that these people didn't even know each other. Turns out that for the past eight years, Fann Beach has become a kind of public gym, where hundreds of strangers congregate to exercise by the shore. Some were jogging, others were doing push-ups, but most were engaged in group aerobics in beautifully choreographed splendor. And what was most uplifting about it was the underlying message: here were people from all walks of life, helping one another, pushing each other to become healthier, stronger, and better. If ever there was the perfect definition of community, this was it.

PART 4
GETTING PERSONAL

AN ENCOUNTER IN JERUSALEM

JEWS VS. ARABS

JERUSALEM, DAY 664

> It is easier to build strong children than to repair broken men.
> —FREDERICK DOUGLASS

One of the many joys of doing Nas Daily was planning the itinerary. I'd decided early on that keeping my destinations unpredictable was an essential ingredient to the concept. Similarly, I was careful not to return to a country I'd already visited unless there was a good reason for it.

Israel was a perfect example of that rule. Over the course of three years, I went home frequently. That's because, like any kid who's moved away, I missed my family; and I figured if I could drop in for a little reunion and a home-cooked meal—while still keeping the show going—why not?

But in January 2018, I made one return trip to Israel that left me feeling more distressed than inspired. I was making a video in an Orthodox Jewish community in Jerusalem, and I'd set up the shot in a secluded alleyway: carved stone walls, decorative cast-iron window gratings, hanging plants everywhere, and overhead, the leafy branch of a lemon tree.

I was in the middle of speaking to the camera when an Orthodox Jew walked up behind me, toward camera and in frame. "Oh, excuse me," he apologized when he saw that I was filming.

"No, no, not at all," I replied. "Go ahead, go ahead. Everything is okay. Hakuna matata!"

This happens a lot when you film in public places, and I was more than happy to let him pass through. But he didn't keep walking. Instead, he stopped to ask me what I was doing. I told him about Nas Daily. He seemed genuinely interested and inquired about my audience and the number of my video views. I thought that was an odd question to come from a middle-aged Orthodox Jew— why would he care about my number of views?—but I cheerfully answered him.

"Right now, seven hundred million," I said.

"No way!" he responded.

Clearly he was impressed—and, from his comments, he apparently knew a thing or two about social media. I was excited about that because he represented a new demographic that I had been wanting to capture. We talked a bit more about the show, and that's when the conversation took a subtle but detectable shift—as it often does in this part of the world. He asked me about my roots.

"I'm Palestinian-Israeli," I said.

"No, really?" he replied, evidently surprised. "But you look . . . you look . . . *intelligent.*"

Uh-oh, I thought, *here it comes.* But I decided to give him the benefit of the doubt and keep things upbeat.

"Well, yes," I said. "But as you must know, most Arabs are your cousins, right?"

"No, no!" he shot back. "I work with many Arabs. They're not intelligent. They're barbaric."

And there it was. In less than two minutes of conversation, this stranger had revealed to me that he firmly believed an entire race—*my* race—was stupid and barbaric. I was speechless.

"Uh, okay," I said. "Um. Thank you so much. I think that . . ."

I honestly couldn't find the words. For one thing, I was having a little trouble conversing with him in his native Hebrew. For another, I was finding it increasingly difficult to stay calm and collected while he personally attacked me and my people—*for no reason.*

But he kept on talking, insisting that I couldn't possibly be Palestinian. And no matter how hard I tried to tell him otherwise, he wouldn't budge. He finally concluded I was French.

It's important to note that this kind of encounter is certainly not a unique interaction between Jews and Arabs in this part of the world. Worse confrontations happen every day. In fact, some are fatal. It's also important to note that there's a flip side to all of this. I've had many private conversations with Arabs who, just like this guy, claim that "all Jews are bad people." Bigotry is an equal-opportunity personality flaw. It doesn't discriminate.

Suddenly a young girl appeared in the alley. The man told me that she was his fifteen-year-old sister. They began talking to each other as if I weren't there.

"Who's that?" she asked her brother, gesturing to me.

"He's just filming," the man told her. "Whatever. He's Palestinian."

"Hello," I said to the girl. "Your brother is right. I'm Palestinian."

In most circumstances, I describe myself as Palestinian-Israeli to anyone who asks. But this time was different. This time I felt it was necessary to emphasize my Palestinian roots. Proudly.

She ignored me and kept talking to her brother. "Why does he act proud of that?" she asked.

"Because he is proud of it," the brother said. "What's the problem? Why not be proud?"

The girl's eye narrowed. "Then why do they kill us?" she said.

I turned in my chair to face her.

"I don't kill anybody," I said. "There are millions of people who don't kill. You don't kill anyone, right? I don't either."

It was surreal—as if, suddenly, the whole world had turned into hate, right there in that little garden alley in Jerusalem. It was one thing to be defending my ethnicity to an adult, but this was a fifteen-year-old Jewish child who lived less than a mile away from Arabs—and apparently she possessed nothing but hate for them. This was a bigger problem.

Until that moment, the girl had been looking past me as she spoke with her brother. Now she faced me, her hands on her hips.

"If it were up to me," she said, "I wouldn't let any Arabs enter this area."

"Why not?" I asked.

"Because they want to kill us."

"You're fifteen years old!" I said. "How do you know all of this?"

"Because 10 percent of Palestinians are terrorists," her brother interjected.

"No," the girl disagreed. "There is no Arab who's not a terrorist."

"I'm not a terrorist," I repeated, "and I'm Arab."

"You're not Arab!" she insisted.

"I *am* Arab!" I said. "I speak Arabic, and I don't want to kill you. I want to be your friend."

"No," she said defiantly. "All Arabs are terrorists!"

And around in a circle we went.

Hate is never fun to feel, but I have to say that receiving it from a fifteen-year-old hurt a little more—especially there in Jerusalem, a city where Jews and Muslims share backyards, dine in the same falafel shops, and pray to their gods in houses of worship that stand side by side. I hurt not just for myself, but for my people.

I'd kept my camera rolling throughout this encounter, and when I got home that night, I watched the footage several times. It took me two weeks to post it—and when I did, I let it run its full five-minute length, rather than cut it down to sixty seconds. As hard as it was to watch, I didn't want to dilute its truth.

The more I've thought about that day in Jerusalem, the less anger I've felt toward that man, his sister, and all who think like them—Jew and Arab alike. This is what they believe because this is all they know. Whenever they turn on their TVs, all they see are Arabs trying to kill Jews and Jews trying to kill Arabs. They don't see that the majority of people have no desire for war—that they work together and go to school together and celebrate their lives together.

This passing incident—this five-minute conversation in a random alley in the holiest city on the most embattled soil on earth—taught me that people like us, you and me, need to be heard more by those who dwell in hatred. We need to be on their TVs and in their magazines and on their Facebook news feeds. We need to reach them in their synagogues and in their mosques. We need to let them know that not all Arabs are terrorists, and not all Jews are bad.

And we need to do this urgently—so that the next time we meet one another in a garden alley, we can talk about something as boring as the weather.

MY JAPANESE FRIEND

JAPAN, DAY 516

There's something about Japan. I can't say for sure why I kept returning to it during my Nas Daily travels, but the lure of the place was pretty intoxicating. I clearly fell in love with the country—and, more to the point, with its people.

By the time I made my second trip to Japan, Nas Daily's audience had grown significantly. I announced my meetup as usual, and more than two hundred people showed up. Frankly, this was two hundred more people than I'd expected, because the Japanese often struggle with English. In fact, it always surprised me that I had such a strong Japanese following on Nas Daily, because all of the videos were in English.

But there they were, two hundred new Japanese friends, all of them happy to participate in the meetup.

One of these people was a young man named Yuki.* He was twenty-three years old, a nice-looking guy—average height, sweet face—and always eager to please. He was also the first person to offer me any help that I might need during my stay in Japan. I typically sought assistance from locals whenever I arrived in a country, and Yuki seemed eager to lend a hand.

I'll admit, however, that my requests for help on this particular trip were somewhat out of the ordinary. For example, I asked Yuki whether he could help me find a place to sleep while I was in the country—outside. By now, I was very familiar with Japan's outrageous prices, so I had decided to make a

---

* Not his real name.

video that expressed my frustration about that: I would sleep on the street. I even convinced Alyne to do the stunt with me. Yuki not only volunteered to help us find the perfect spot, he was also the only person at the meetup to offer to spend the night *with* us—and all so I could illustrate my dumb point. I was impressed by that. I liked Yuki.

The video was well received, and the next day I continued to look for other important topics to cover. And I found a pretty potent one. Turns out that the insane cost of living isn't the only runaway problem Japan has to worry about. The country also suffers frighteningly high rates of stress and depression. When I first learned about that, I was surprised. How could anybody be depressed in Japan? It's an amazing place to live and prosper. It's polite, clean, safe, smart—practically perfect.

And yet that very pursuit of perfection—that relentless drive to succeed—has a hidden cost. And that led me to explore the one place in Japan I will never be able to shake: the Suicide Forest.

Located on the northwestern flank of Mount Fuji, sixty miles west of Tokyo, the Aokigahara forest (also known as the Sea of Trees) is a thirteen-square-mile plot of dense woods that, like everything else in Japan, is staggeringly

AOKIGAHARA, "THE SUICIDE FOREST"

pretty. Electric-green broadleaf trees sprout from its floor of volcanic rock, creating a cool canopy for the wildlife that roams there—from Asian black bears and Japanese mink to bats and beetles and butterflies.

But it is the unending wave of human sadness that persistently streams into this quiet woodland that gives the forest its tragic nickname. As many as a hundred people take their own lives in the Suicide Forest every year, a phenomenon so chronic that officials have placed signs at the forest's entrance urging those with fatal intentions to seek help instead.

But they just keep coming, on and on, hiking through the thick foliage until they're lost in its shadows. They sometimes trail a plastic ribbon behind them so they can find their way out if they change their mind. Oftentimes, they don't. Most end their lives by hanging; others overdose on drugs or ingest poison. Either way, their last moments are undoubtedly draped in crushing silence. The trees in the forest are so closely spaced that not even the wind can be heard; and because the soil is rich with magnetic iron, cell phone signals are often disrupted, making any last, desperate pleas for help nearly impossible. Some have called the depths of the Suicide Forest "a chasm of emptiness."

Of course, suicide is not new to Japan—*seppuku* (or *harakiri*) dates back to the country's feudal era in the twelfth century, when samurai warriors or shamed commoners would end their lives to restore honor to themselves or their families. Today, this ritual is less about honor than it is an expression of hopelessness. While in recent years, Japan's annual suicide rate has reached all-time lows, it is still among the highest in the world—at sixty deaths a day, nearly twice the rate of Germany—and has subsequently become an issue of national urgency.

I didn't hesitate for one moment to make a video about the Suicide Forest. Raising awareness is never a bad thing, especially when so many people are suffering. In fact, when I was editing the video on Day 516, I decided to include Japanese subtitles so that I could reach as many people as possible. And whatever private concerns I may have harbored about raising such a dire topic were instantly dispelled when the comments started rolling in. The video had clearly struck a nerve.

"Thank you for covering such a taboo subject," one follower wrote. "The stigma around mental illness is harmful and polarizing. But maybe with videos like this, we can start to let others know that it's okay to ask for help." Many agreed.

I was grateful that the video had spoken intimately to so many people. What surprised me, however, was that one of those people was my new Japanese friend, Yuki. He'd recently had his own brush with suicide, he confided to me, and he barely escaped by the roll of the dice. Literally.

When he told me this, I thought he was kidding—or at the very least, that I wasn't understanding him properly because of some translation error. But Yuki wasn't joking, and when he shared the details of his story, I was floored. I asked him if he'd be willing to tell it again, this time on camera.

He agreed—but only with his identity hidden. So we put a gray scarf around his face and a Santa Claus cap on his head and we didn't reveal his name. Then he told his story:

Just the month before, he said, he had lost the appetite to live any longer and sank so deeply into despair that he began planning his death. But one tiny part of him wasn't entirely sure about this decision, so he gave himself an out: for seven nights in a row, he would roll a single die to determine his fate. If it landed on the number six, he would end his life; if not, he would abandon the plan.

That first night, the six did not appear. Nor did it appear on the second and third nights, or the fourth, fifth, and sixth. On the seventh night, he rolled the die and looked down at the number.

Four.

He called off the plan, escaping death by sheer luck.

After we finished shooting the video, I hugged Yuki and thanked him for his candor. When I posted the video a few hours later, millions of viewers expressed their support of him. The outpouring was astonishing. And just as I'd expected, Yuki was following those comments closely. In fact, later that evening, he texted me, telling me that he truly felt loved. I was so gratified to hear that, as this was my objective all along: To make him feel loved. To convince him that millions of people cared about him. To implore him never to consider taking his life again.

And yet I still felt uneasy. This was a young man, practically a boy, for whom suicide seemed the unlikeliest of choices. He had a good family, a good job, adequate money, and close friends. Would he fall back into the same dark place in a few weeks? Days? Hours?

MY FRIEND YUKI

I left Japan a couple of days later, harboring more questions than answers. But the one thing I did know is that life is hard, especially in Japan, a society in which people endure extraordinary pressure every day—about their jobs, their income, their social status, their grades in school. Is this why the Suicide Forest still exists? Will more Japanese men and women continue to roll dice in the darkness?

In the case of my young friend, yes. Nine months after I shot his video, I texted Yuki just to check in. This was something that Alyne and I tried to do regularly, because we worried about him. We had hoped to invite him to travel with us and celebrate the end of Nas Daily together. We really cared for him.

But when he didn't respond to our messages, we grew uneasy. And then we learned the shocking news. Just a few weeks earlier, Yuki had taken his life without reaching out for help. He'd rolled the die again, and this time it came up six.

I was thunderstruck by the news. Devastated. It made me angry at myself for not checking in more often and even angrier for assuming that Yuki was okay. He was not okay.

Since Day 201 of Nas Daily, I'd worn a T-shirt designed to reveal the percentages of life: how long we've been here and, statistically speaking, how much time we have left. In addition to the many things Japan taught me during my travels there—about beauty and pride, endurance and hard work—it also taught me that sometimes the T-shirt lies.

In the thousands of hours I shot for Nas Daily, this was one of the few stories that made me cry.

If you or someone you know is considering suicide, please contact the National Suicide Prevention Lifeline at 1-800-273-TALK (8255).

THE NUMBERS TRAP

Imagine you have a bank account, and every day I give you 5 euros to deposit into it. The first day you'd be happy. The second day you'd be happy. You might even be happy for a whole week. But very quickly you'd start to grow less happy—because sooner or later you'd begin thinking, "Gee, 50 *euros* a day would make me so much happier!"

See what happened? Suddenly, 5 euros doesn't cut it anymore. Why? Because you're stuck in "the Numbers Trap."

This is the trap that many of my friends and I fall into all the time, and it actually has nothing to do with money—but everything to do with numbers.

Whether we know it or not, we humans derive a lot of our happiness from numbers. They satisfy us. They drive us. They help us *quantify* our feelings. And, naturally, the higher the number, the better we feel.

The more Instagram likes you get, the more accepted you feel.

The more goals your football team scores, the happier you are.

And, of course, the more money you make, the better life gets.

But here's the kicker: *numbers never end.*

So in theory, this means two things: (1) you can always get higher numbers and feel even happier, but (2) because the ceiling keeps rising, you'll never reach full happiness.

Welcome to the Numbers Trap.

When I first realized this, I was shocked, then annoyed, then devastated. That's because, like many others, I attach my concept of success—and happiness—to these never-ending numbers. I noticed this especially when I started Nas Daily.

Number of likes.

Number of followers.

Number of friends.

Number of video views.

Number of dollars.

Even when my audience crossed over into the millions, I celebrated for about five minutes before I began thinking, *Why not ten million? Why not a billion?*

This is the Numbers Trap on crack—when even billions don't make you happy.

Bob Marley understood the Numbers Trap, and he warned us about it. "Money is numbers, and numbers never end," he once said. "If it takes money to be happy, your search for happiness will never end."

Thanks to Bob (and my girlfriend, and my family), I gradually came to understand that happiness is not something you can count on your fingers; and that the only numbers we should really care about are how many people we have in our lives, how often we get to see them, and (if we really work hard at this) how many hearts we can touch.

I can't claim that I'm very good at this yet—I'm still in the process of rewiring my brain. But I'm trying.

COMING HOME

I write these words as I listen to the moving music of Fairuz, a beloved artist who for fifty years has captured the souls of Arabs all across the Middle East. The song playing at this moment is called "Zahrat al-Madaen," or "The Flower of All Cities."

Our eyes gaze toward you every day as we pray
They gaze about the halls of the temples
They behold the ancient churches
They wipe away the sadness from the mosques

The song is an homage to Jerusalem, which Fairuz has called her favorite city. She is not alone. Jerusalem is my favorite city, too. It is the holiest, most inspiring, most wondrous city I have ever visited. It captured my heart the first time I stepped inside its walls.

"You are obligated to visit Jerusalem before you die," I told my friends in college. "This city has something for everyone." I wasn't exaggerating. If you're Jewish, the Temple Mount is right there for you in Jerusalem. If you're Christian, Jesus's tomb is in Jerusalem. If you're Muslim, the Al-Aqsa mosque is in the heart of Jerusalem. If you're an atheist, well, the nightclubs of Jerusalem are pretty cool.

No other city in the world so sacredly brings these three religions together in one place. Not one.

JERUSALEM: "OUR EYES GAZE TOWARD YOU EVERY DAY"

I was just five years old when my fascination with Jerusalem was first ignited. I vividly recall walking through the Old City. To my left was an Orthodox Jew, to my right was an orthodox Muslim, and in front of me was a Christian priest. All three seemed comfortable within their respective faiths, mindful of the others' religion while practicing quietly their own. I was just a little boy, but I recognized that there was something magical about that. And as I grew, the magic grew along with me.

I visited Jerusalem on several occasions throughout Nas Daily, and even when I wasn't there, I frequently talked about it. But each time I did—despite my affection for the city—the cold reality of Jerusalem became harder and harder to ignore: that it is stuck in a deadly continuum. In fact, I'm convinced that if all religions of the world suddenly called for peace with one another, there would still be fighting in Jerusalem. It's the way the city lives.

Case in point: On Day 469, I'd just wrapped up a two-week swing through Brazil and decided to drop in at home in Israel before heading to my next destination. I figured it would be fun to ambush my parents with a little surprise visit and film their reactions. But the surprise was on me: Mom and Dad were out of the country.

That was okay, though. As disappointed as I was at not seeing them, I hadn't gotten very much alone time over the previous year. So I showered, made a sandwich, and grabbed a beer, then checked my phone for the latest news.

Not a good idea. There on my little screen was a stream of unsettling, all-too-familiar images—the ones I'd grown up seeing: soldiers and civilians tearing through the streets of my favorite city. Smoke-bomb canisters arcing through the air. Fists being thrown and bodies being kicked. Jerusalem was essentially at war.

The casualties were dire: three Palestinian teenagers had been shot and killed that morning, and then later in the day, three Israelis had been stabbed to death in retaliation. This was becoming the new normal in Jerusalem, and it was hard to ignore, especially when innocent lives were being wasted.

The conflict had begun one week earlier on the morning of July 14 in the Old City. Three men armed with pistols and improvised submachine guns had stormed out of the Temple Mount—the three-thousand-year-old plaza that is arguably the holiest sanctuary in all of Christianity, Judaism, and Islam—and exited the square's gates, their weapons blazing. They shot at the Israeli Border Police officers who were stationed there, then retreated back into the compound and positioned themselves in front of the mosque. Gunfire followed and all three attackers were killed. Two Israeli officers died as well.

In the wake of the ambush, the Old City was closed to traffic. For the first time in decades, the Temple Mount was shut down by Israeli authorities, and Friday prayers at the Al-Aqsa mosque were canceled. The Israelis conducted raids and interrogations for the next two days, ultimately reopening the Temple Mount with metal detectors at its gates.

That security measure—a checkpoint at the entrance of a holy place—lit the fuse, and hundreds of Arab protestors swarmed into the area for the next week. Israeli and Palestinian political leaders entered the fray, and the violent clashes spilled into the surrounding regions. The anger and tension finally boiled over on July 21, just as I was crossing the ocean from Brazil for my surprise homecoming. The three Palestinian youths—two of them eighteen years old and the other one nineteen—were shot and killed during demonstrations in the occupied West Bank and Gaza. Later that day, a nineteen-year-old Palestinian broke into the home of an Israeli settlement family during their Sabbath dinner and stabbed three of them to death.

This is what I came home to.

This is what has gone on for millennia.

People often ask me, "Why is there always violence in Jerusalem?" and I always say the same thing: that as crazy as it sounds, it's really about love.

THE "IMMOVABLE" LADDER

I'm not being glib. Jews, Muslims, and Christians love this city so deeply that they are willing to die for it. And any change to Jerusalem—a metal detector installed in front of a place of worship, even a water bottle placed on the cobblestones—will cause turbulence in this sacred place.

Indeed, to understand the deep-seated protectiveness Christians, Muslims, and Jews feel for Jerusalem, you need look no further than the ladder that stands beneath a window in the Church of the Holy Sepulchre. It was left there in the eighteenth century by a mason who was doing restoration work on the church. It is now called "immovable" because no single cleric of the six Christian orders that pray there is permitted to alter any part of church property without the permission of the other five. No surprise, that ladder has never budged.

And these are just Christians fighting among themselves. Throw Jews and Muslims into the mix, and you've got a city that is always teetering on the razor's edge of calamity. And from calamity comes violence. And from violence comes death.

And that's the painful truth of Jerusalem—the love and violence swing back and forth like a tragic pendulum. Even the song I began listening to as I sat down to write this has suddenly shifted, in real time, from a peaceful melody to one of defiance. "The great anger is coming," Fairuz sings now, underscoring the Arab world's undying determination to one day reclaim Jerusalem from the Jews.

As I listen to the song, the five-year-old boy who lives inside of me still can't grasp the deep divide within the holy walls of Jerusalem. Despite the images he sees on his television, he's still trying to hold on to that magic.

But I think he's beginning to catch on. In this world, there is precious little that I wouldn't give to see the city I love most thrive in peace—because I am convinced that the moment peace prevails in Jerusalem, it will prevail everywhere in the world.

But until then, as I told my viewers the first time I took them to that remarkable city: "Don't die before visiting Jerusalem. Just make sure not to die there."

It was every traveler's worst nightmare. In 2011, while on vacation in Cyprus, Dawn Foote lost her precious cat. Like any pet owner, she immediately set out on a frantic search for him, but no matter where she went on the lush Mediterranean island, she saw no sign of her little whiskered friend. What she did find, however, were dozens of stray cats—some hiding out beneath cars in parking lots, others wandering about the island's tropical foliage. And in the worst cases, many of these cats were in poor health from living alone in the wild—some suffering infections, others bearing the scars of encounters with hunting dogs. Dawn's heart broke for these lost animals, so she made a life-changing decision. Instead of buying a beach house with her retirement money, she packed up her home in the UK and relocated to Cyprus, where she opened a giant cat sanctuary—Tala Monastery Cats. There, hordes of homeless kitties are cleaned, fed, cared for, and put up for adoption. On the day I spent at Tala, Dawn and her passionate team of volunteers were playing host to more than eight hundred cats, each one of them adorable, healthy, and, most important, safe. I even wound up sponsoring a cat for just 50 euros per year. And what did I name him? Nas Daily, of course—because he was a pretty cool cat.

ETHIOPIA HYENA MAN

Let's be clear about one thing: hyenas are deadly predators. With their strong jaws and daggerlike teeth, they're capable of ripping a human to pieces and never looking back. But twenty-six-year-old Abbas Yusuf of Ethiopia—known throughout his remote village as Hyena Man—has got the wild beasts eating out of his hand. Literally. Hyenas are a common sight in the walled city of Harar, especially at night when they prowl the alleys and landfills looking for something meaty to drag back to their caves. But the smarter ones make a beeline for the dirt yard outside Abbas's home, where he's happy to feed them goodies he's picked up at the local meat market. The hyenas totally dig it, frolicking and cuddling with Abbas when they're not too busy chowing down. Abbas is on a first-name basis with all the members of the pack (he picks names based on their looks and personality—Lazy, Hairy, Skinny), and he's actually become a tourist

attraction, mostly for his signature trick: holding a stick between his teeth with a scrap of meat dangling from it and then letting the hyenas gently nibble at it. But Abbas's feeding routine is no mere stunt—it's actually a family tradition that reaches back four generations. He learned the trade from his dad, whom he credits for taming the hyena homeys. "After my father started feeding them," he told me, "they never again attacked the people of Harar." In a world of conflict like ours, it was inspiring to watch Abbas being so chill with a bunch of fanged carnivores. If they can get along, maybe there's hope for the rest of us.

THE WORLD **THE BIGGEST (FREE) UNIVERSITY ON THE PLANET**

Not many people think big, but those who do are the ones who move mountains. One of those heady dreamers is Shai Reshef, a sixty-four-year-old educational entrepreneur who revolutionized the way the world thinks about learning. In 2008, Shai crunched a few numbers and determined that, around the globe, a hundred million students were unable to attend a university, despite their intelligence or motivation. The problem? Either they had no money, tuitions were too high, or schools had no space for them. Refusing to accept that anyone should be denied a quality education, Shai decided to fix the system with a simple four-step plan. *One:* Building campuses costs money, so put the college online. *Two:* Professors cost money, so hire volunteers to teach. *Three:* Enrollment costs money, so don't charge tuition. *Four:* Textbooks cost money, so digitize the books and put them on the web—for free. The only expense for students, Shai decided, would be a simple $100 fee for taking an exam ("and even then," he told me, "if you can't pay,

then that's free, too"). Shai named his brainchild the University of the People, and from the moment he flipped the on switch, the idea caught fire. Seven thousand academics—including professors from Harvard and New York University—reached out to volunteer; foundations stepped forward to donate funds; and thousands of students from around the globe sat down, logged on, and signed up for the world's first nonprofit, tuition-free, accredited online university. And what a student body they are: teenagers, stay-at-home moms, seniors, the homeless, Syrian refugees, genocide survivors, and countless others from two hundred countries who otherwise can't afford an education. After the university racked up eighteen thousand students, Shai's goal became building a system that works for a hundred million more—at long last making education not a privilege but a human right. "If you educate one person," Shai says, "you can change a life. But if you educate many, you can change the world."

MOROCCO **THE CITY THAT'S ALL BLUE**

Blue, blue, blue, blue, blue! It's one thing for a city to have a recurring color palette; it's another thing when the place is wall-to-wall blue. Still, as you step onto the fabled streets of Chefchaouen—a quaint stone township tucked in the hills of northern Morocco—you'll find yourself instantly smiling at its charming color coordination. The city was built as a casbah, or fortress, in 1471, to protect its inhabitants from the invading Portuguese; but the paintbrushes didn't come out for another twenty years. The reason for all that blue is still speculative. Some say the Jewish settlers fleeing the Spanish Inquisition brought the color with them as a symbol of God's power, then gave the city a fresh coat of it in the 1930s. Others say the blue serves a much more practical purpose: to keep the mosquitoes away. Whatever its true origins, the most popular party line is that the blue is a reflection of heaven that reminds us to live a spiritual life. However, often left unmentioned in the travel brochures are the ample patches of *green* found in the surrounding mountains—specifically, the cannabis plantations that produce primo hashish for locals and visitors. When I made my trip to Chefchaouen on Day 358, I thought it was important to mention this—so I came up with an unofficial slogan for the place. "Chefchaouen!" I said. "Come for the blue and stay for the green."

INDIA **THE CITY THAT'S ALL PINK**

Pink, pink, pink, pink, pink! I never would have thought a color as sweet as pink could be bossy, but in Jaipur—the capital city of India's northern state of Rajasthan—the cotton-candy color scheme is actually mandated by local law. Technically more terracotta than flamingo, Jaipur's signature pinkness made its debut in 1876, when the city was paid a visit by Prince Albert Edward of Wales, the eldest son of Queen Victoria. Eager to impress the royal tourist, Jaipur's powerful Maharaja Ram Singh II ordered the border-to-border paint job, and pink was picked as the most hospitable hue. After the prince split, the Maharaja's wife hinted to him—as spouses often do—that she loved the city's bubblegum makeover and would be super happy if the color remained. So the law was laid down. It's worth noting that a century before its pinkification, the city didn't even exist. It had been built from scratch—in just four years—as the new capital, and it used a grid system not unlike New York City's. Builders also took care to design the overlooking Hawa Mahal palace so that the royal ladies could watch the street festivals below and not be seen. Why? So they wouldn't have to wear their veils.

PART 5
CONFLICT

LET YOUR HAIR DOWN

THE MALDIVES, DAY 771

Amazingly, the entire video was only 172 words long—and I spoke 130 of them. That means that X* said just 42 words—and if you discount her last 6 ("That's one minute, see you tomorrow!"), we're down to 36.

The fact that three dozen words should stir up such vitriol, such condemnation, such *hate* still blows my mind.

But, of course, it wasn't the words that got X into trouble. It was the ten-second clip of her showing her hair.

I had arrived in the Republic of Maldives six days earlier and was instantly charmed. And who wouldn't be? A garland of twelve hundred coral islands gently strung across the equator in the Indian Ocean, just southwest of Sri Lanka, the Maldives looks like a living brochure for heaven. In fact, "heaven" is exactly how I described this tropical paradise. "Once you visit the Maldives," I observed, "you will want to become a better person, just so you can go to heaven again in the afterlife and relive the experience."

I met X on my second day on the islands. I was in a public square, shooting the local meetup, and X was among the hundreds of young Maldivians who had come to say hello. Like most of the women there, she was wearing a traditional hijab—a garment worn by many women of the Muslim faith. Technically, the hijab is a simple veil that covers the head, shoulders, and upper chest; but in religious terms, it's more than a cultural fashion accessory.

---

* I identify the young woman discussed here as "X"—just as I did in her Nas Daily video—in order to protect her identity.

In the Islamic scriptures, the Quran, both men and women are instructed to dress modestly, with the hijab serving as a kind of spiritual partition that separates the wrongdoers from the righteous, the believers from the nonbelievers. But once you get a little deeper into the Quran's text, it is women who bear the brunt of the dress code.

"Women . . . should lower their gaze and guard their private parts," the Quran commands, eventually zeroing in on the breasts as the part of the anatomy most in need of concealment.

As a Muslim, I have no problem with hijabs—most of the women in my family wear one—but what sets my teeth on edge is women being forced to wear them when they don't want to. In Saudi Arabia, Iran, and parts of Indonesia, women are required by law to dress in a hijab; and in strict Muslim communities, all women must wear the hijab when they are in the presence of any male outside of their immediate family. I believe wearing a hijab should be a choice, not a law.

Which brings us back to X. During our Nas Daily meetup, I began discussing her hijab with her, telling her that just nine months earlier I'd interviewed a Muslim woman in the Philippines who'd proudly defended her own veil. "It helps me feel closer to God," the woman had told me. I asked X if she felt the same way.

X

"No," she said emphatically. "I want to show my hair."

X told me that she'd been wearing a hijab since she was thirteen. All of her classmates covered their hair, and she'd felt pressured to do the same. Her parents hadn't forced her to put on the veil, X said, but society had. "And once you cover your hair," she told me, "it's much harder to uncover it without getting in trouble."

There was also the impracticality of wearing a hijab in the Maldives, X said. The islands are always hot and often humid. The last thing you need is an extra layer of clothing over your skin.

The irony of X's dilemma didn't escape me. Here was this bright, articulate Muslim woman, who at age twenty-four lived in a religious culture that permitted her to talk on a cell phone, have a boyfriend, even divorce a husband, if she had one—all of the freedoms one hopes an ancient religion will grant as it adapts to modern times. But removing a hijab wasn't considered a freedom—it was a defiance, and one that carried personal risk.

"I'm afraid people will judge me," X said, "but I just feel like taking it off."

I asked X whether she wanted to do that on camera for Nas Daily. I told her we could cover her face with a niqab (a Muslim hood that conceals everything but the eyes), that we wouldn't reveal her name, and that I'd be sure to shoot her against generic backdrops to further protect her identity. I also warned her that, should she agree, there was bound to be a backlash online.

"Yes," X said, "I want to do this."

So we began.

In terms of technical execution, the video wasn't very complicated. It opens with a shot of X, wearing a turquoise niqab, staring straight into the camera. Behind her is a patch of bright-green Maldivian flora. If nothing else, it's a lovely image.

We then proceed to tell X's story. She speaks to the camera throughout, and we follow her as she walks along a beach and talks on her cell phone. I zoom in to a close-up on her hands as she reaches beneath her chin and begins untying the knot of her niqab.

Finally, she gracefully slides the niqab from her head, revealing for the first time her thick black hair. I was surprised at how long and lustrous it was. It was also undeniably beautiful. At one point, I catch X from the side as she runs her fingers through her hair. Her face is still concealed, but you can see from the subtle rise of her cheek that she's smiling.

After the shoot, I thanked X for her bravery. We exchanged phone numbers so that we could stay in touch. I returned to my hotel to edit the video and add my voice-over. I ended the script with one line of commentary I thought important to underscore:

> This is the story of one woman out of many who didn't grow any more or less religious—she just wanted to show her hair.

I posted the video at 7:00 a.m. Ordinarily, I do not dictate to my viewers how to respond to any given post—that's not my right. In this case, however, I wrote a cautionary note:

> This is a sensitive topic for many, especially for X. That's why her face and identity are covered. I'm sure this will result in lots of comments. My only request is to keep it polite and respectful.

The response was almost instantaneous, as the first of more than nine thousand comments came pouring in. My initial feelings were of relief, as my community began expressing its support. "Hi, X," wrote an African woman named Chichi, "I'm sorry you have to hide your identity to speak your truth. I just want to let you know that, even though I do not know you, I love you and sincerely believe that you and every other woman in your predicament should be free to live her life as she so pleases. Love from Nigeria xo"

But the well-wishes and good vibes were short-lived. Some viewers were critical of X for defying her faith; others defended the rituals of Islam; most took me to task for making the video in the first place. "Religion is a much bigger topic than your small brain can understand," one man posted. "You showed your true colors with this video. I thought you were a better person than this."

That stung. I've gotten my fair share of insults and name-calling, but the suggestion that I had no authority to address this particular subject was a low blow. "Stick to travel videos." "Don't interfere in religious issues." Gratuitous digs like those implied that I had treaded into a discussion I knew nothing about.

Which was preposterous. I am a Muslim. I am an Arab. And just three days earlier, I had posted a video from the Maldives honoring the often over-looked grace of Ramadan.

"Think about this," I'd said. "Almost two billion people agree that for this month you should try to be a better human, to learn humility and patience, and feel for the hungry and the poor. So let's celebrate as a community. This is a big part of the Muslim culture that sadly goes unnoticed as the media focuses on what's bad. But as 24 percent of the world celebrates Ramadan, try to join them."

And now this shit.

But my personal anger over the negative comments was secondary to my concern for X's safety. As I'd most feared, within the next few days media outlets somehow identified her home island, and she began getting harassed. Police interrogated her mother. And newspapers started running tabloid-like stories about X, claiming that she'd been forced to flee her island. None of that was true.

Still, it all became too much. So I pulled the plug. I blocked the video in the Maldives. I'd never banned one of my videos before. "Dear Nas Daily community," I explained on Facebook, "it is with a heavy heart that I blocked this video from showing in the Maldives, but I wanted to protect the person who appears in it. Please respond with encouraging comments to make X feel better. As you can tell from this backlash, it's a very sensitive topic. Let's make X feel supported instead of defeated."

Hundreds of new comments streamed in, most of them positive, and the hateful messages eventually died down. I shot in the Maldives for a few more days, but even as I moved on to Sri Lanka, I couldn't quite shake the feeling of sadness about what had transpired. The uproar hadn't made me lose faith in Nas Daily, as much as it made me lose faith in humanity.

Looking back, however, I wouldn't have done anything differently. It was right to make the video. It was right to block it. I just wish it hadn't been weaponized by some to advance their own hate.

I checked in on X occasionally, and she was doing fine. As for me, I remained melancholy for about a week. But then I remembered a favorite bit of wisdom that I'd once read in the Quran: "Show forgiveness, enjoin what is good, and turn away from the ignorant."

I took that advice.

WHAT IS CHINESE WATER TORTURE?

Today, I did a little experiment. I took a plastic water bottle, sliced a small slit in its cap, then laid it on a table so that its neck extended over the edge. Then I got on my back beneath the table and let the water drip onto my forehead, droplet by droplet. This is what is known as the "Chinese Water Torture," an interrogation technique that dates back to the fifteenth century. It was allegedly used in China to get information from a victim before he went totally insane.

There's a lot of debate over whether this method of torture was actually ever implemented—by the Chinese or others—but that wasn't the point of my exercise. What I was trying to replicate was the way in which a series of tiny, harmless annoyances can ultimately drive a person nuts.

Everyone has personal peeves. We typically call them "small issues." Women hate sitting down on a toilet only to fall into the water because the dude who was there before her left the seat up. Most people are secretly bugged when a friend reaches over to their plate and grabs a French fry. And everyone despises robocalls.

But none of these irks are life-threatening, and all of them can be easily fixed: put the seat down yourself, smack your friend's hand, and don't answer the damn phone.

Or you can just let it all go.

But here's where it gets interesting. If enough of these small disturbances start to pile up—one maddening drop after another, for days on end—you will eventually blow. Small stress points, like small droplets of water, can be quite powerful.

I've noticed this phenomenon in my commitment to Nas Daily. After 786 days of writing, shooting, editing, and posting my videos—once a day for more than two years—I'm starting to break. The smallest things now put me over the edge. Like the way my computer desktop is so cluttered with video files that I can't find what I'm looking for. Or the way the letter *i* sticks on my keypad, and I practically have to whack it with a hammer to get my laptop to recognize it. Or the torturously *slooowww* response rate of my editing software. The dripping never seems to stop, and at some point, I just lose it.

In the interest of full disclosure, I should add that Alyne doesn't make things any easier. "Let's take a picture here, Poopie," she'll tell me while we're walking down the street—which, of course, wouldn't be irritating, if she didn't ask me to take another picture on the next block, and the block after that, and so on.

And I'm no different. If I accidentally step on her foot while we're on the bus, fine, she doesn't even mention it. But when I do it five times a day, five days in a row, she eventually snaps—and rightfully so.

Drip, drip, drip . . .

I stopped my little water-torture experiment after just a few minutes, but had I let it continue, I probably wouldn't have lasted more than half an hour before leaping to my feet, screaming, and throwing the water bottle against the wall—those water droplets can really add up! But here's what I learned from the exercise:

Although, at this moment, none of us is literally lying beneath a table with water dripping on our foreheads (at least I hope you're not), many of us *are* suffering the relentless drip-drip-drip of daily stress, and we feel like we're on the verge of cracking. That's because we think these chronic annoyances are out of our control.

But the truth is, they're really not—and they're easy to fix. Take ten minutes to tidy your desktop. Get your keyboard repaired. Take a break from Instagram. And stop stepping on people's feet! Because the more we relieve ourselves—and others—of these petty irritants, the more space we have in our brains for the real challenges in our lives—like career, money, family, and love.

I ended this video with an on-screen message for whoever was watching, but mostly for myself:

Focus on the Big Things
Be Careful of the Small Things

I VISITED A WAR ZONE

THE PHILIPPINES, DAY 492

Let me ask you a question. If someone knocked on your door right now and said, "We are ISIS, and we are taking over your city," what would you do? Would you slam the door? Would you say, "Come on in, let me take your coat?" Or would you not have the slightest idea what to do?

This is a question that, for some strange reason, I've thought about a lot. I've always been fascinated by the rise of terrorism, particularly ISIS (the Islamic State of Iraq and the Levant). How could something so brutal, so destructive, so primitive gain such a deadly foothold in certain parts of the world? Why does it happen? How does it happen? And most pressing, who does it affect the most?

These are difficult questions, and while I was traveling the world with Nas Daily—especially in areas of conflict—the topic was always in the back of my mind, like a mental Post-it note. Nas Daily was all about humanity, and terrorism is the dark side of humanity. So I knew I had to cover the subject in some way.

But how do you do that? It's not like you can stroll into a city, grab a guidebook, and find the TERRORISTS section somewhere between RESTAURANTS and MUSEUMS. I'd have to wait for a situation to arise.

And arise it did, in August 2017, when ISIS combatants seized the city of Marawi in the Philippines.

Contrary to a popular misconception, ISIS is not a "state," as its name implies. It's a state of mind, an ugly ideology, and unfortunately, that powerful hatred quickly infected thousands in Syria and Iraq. But by the summer of 2017, ISIS had also proved that its crazed doctrine of violence was mobile—mobile enough to hop eighty-six hundred miles across the globe to the South Pacific.

That's why I went to Marawi. I was there to see ISIS up-close.

My plane touched down at Ninoy Aquino International Airport in Manila on Day 482. It had been seven months since I'd first visited the country. Technically, I was there to work on my media company, which I'd been building for several months. I'd brought along a few colleagues, and we took advantage of the affordable prices I'd discovered in Manila the first time around. We stayed at a nice little hotel in the middle of the city and rented a small, clean office just down the street—and all for a fraction of the price we'd have paid for some mediocre Airbnb in San Francisco, where most people launch media companies. I began to understand firsthand why so many American corporations build their businesses overseas.

But then the call came in from a friend, alerting us to the fighting in Marawi, five hundred miles to the south.

MARAWI UNDER SIEGE

The backstory to the ISIS siege was complicated. At the time of our visit, Marawi was in the throes of a violent, five-month conflict between the Philippine government and gangs of radical Islamic terrorists, including Filipino jihadists who had sworn allegiance to ISIS. They'd attacked the city three months earlier, then captured it, vowing to raise the black ISIS flag over its capitol building and establish an Islamic state right there in the middle of the peaceful Philippines. When I'd read about ISIS before this, I'd reflexively thought of Iraq and Syria, never imaging that the violence and hate would spread to the South Pacific. And yet the Marawi siege was—and remains—the longest urban battle in the modern history of the Philippines.

I'd dodged armed conflict before (remember where I grew up), but going to Marawi was a dangerous gamble. Over the course of the siege, hundreds of terrorist guerrillas had ransacked and destroyed homes and hospitals; set fire to a Catholic cathedral, an elementary school, and a college; and even taken a local priest and churchgoers hostage. They interrogated Christians and executed those who could not recite from Islam's holy Quran. I'd never taken Nas Daily to a place like this before, quite honestly because my mother watched every video and I knew she'd worry.

But this trip was important to me. My feel-good videos notwithstanding, I wanted Nas Daily to be more than just eye-candy drone shots or upbeat tourism vignettes. Filipinos were suffering in Marawi, and I wanted to share their stories in a way that was more visual—more real—than the random repurposed articles you'd find on the internet.

I called my friend Jay, who agreed to make the trip with me. We coordinated with the Philippine Army, secured our press passes, and boarded a flight to Ozamiz City in the south. Once there, we donned bulletproof vests and took a two-hour taxi ride—through many checkpoints—to get to Marawi. When we arrived, there was no mistaking that we were in the right place. The horizon was streaked with smoke from air strikes, and gunfire crackled in the air.

I'd spoken to the Nas Daily camera more than five hundred times at that point, but now I felt strangely self-conscious. I didn't want to come off as some hotdog vlogger, pretending he was on the front lines of some hellish armed conflict in Afghanistan, when in fact I was relatively safe. Indeed, Jay and I were following all of the proper safety protocols and stayed in the safe zones controlled by the government forces.

But at the same time, I knew that the video looked dangerous because it *was* dangerous. Bullets were flying, and we needed to be conscious at all times to avoid any stray shots.

I tried to articulate my feelings to my viewers. "This whole effort is not for the views or the likes or even the one-minute video," I said. "None of that shit is worth the risk. We're here because oftentimes during war, stories are born—stories of hardship and sacrifice, love and peace—and we want to give you a glimpse of what it's like to really be here, and maybe find some hope among the hopeless. Wish us luck."

That last part was no exaggeration. On our second day in Marawi, government forces bombed the ISIS outposts and exchanged gunfire with them. We caught all of that on camera. As we made our way through the streets, we saw the damage that had been inflicted over the course of the siege. What used to be a Muslim-majority city was now a ghost town, reduced to abandoned homes and empty streets littered with shell casings from stray bullets. The conflict had left many people homeless or dead—and that was the most heartbreaking part. More than 180,000 peaceful Filipinos had been forced to flee their homes or risk being murdered like many of their friends had been. These were people who had never approved of ISIS, and they certainly didn't invite them to invade their city and lay waste to it.

I was amazed by how relentlessly ISIS fought. But I was equally surprised by the steely conviction of the people who were there to fight back. On my second day in Marawi I met Norodin (Nor) Lucman, a sixty-one-year-old Muslim clan leader and former politician who just a few months earlier had been thrust into the crosshairs of the Marawi siege in an astonishing way.

Nor was in his house in the city when the fighting had first erupted. He ran outside to see what was happening and then spotted a group of men—carpenters and builders—working construction on a nearby house. He quickly ushered them into his home, along with his own employees, to get them out of harm's way. Once inside, he counted heads: there were seventy-four of them altogether, and forty-four were Christian. Leaving the house would be certain death.

Nor assumed the fighting would die down after a day or two and that all of them could then evacuate to safety. But the gunfire continued, and after twelve days, he grew desperate. Although they'd been rationing food and supplies, they'd run out of water, and Nor knew it was time to get out. By then, families from other neighborhoods—men, women, and kids—had also sought shelter in his home; so to prepare the Christians for their escape, Nor taught them the Islamic words of praise for God—"Allahu Akbar"—just to be safe.

At dawn, they all left the house, and, joining up with another local politician who'd hidden dozens of Christians in his own home, Nor led 144 people through the streets of downtown Marawi, witnessing for the first time the decaying corpses of those who'd been killed in battle. The women covered their heads with hijabs, the men carried the children—and no one dared look up at the snipers who were perched on rooftops. Ultimately, Nor and his terrified evacuees made it to safety, in part because the militant soldier at the final checkpoint recognized Nor as a respected Muslim leader from the community and let the group pass.

It was a heart-stopping story of bravery and compassion, but for Nor, the daring rescue was not about heroism. As a scholar who had studied Islam in Mecca and Cairo—at one point Osama bin Laden was his classmate—Nor insisted that he was simply adhering to Islamic teachings that no one person's life is more valuable than another's.

"The Quran instructs us to protect those of other religions as an equal part of humanity," he told me. "We were taught that Muslims and Christians are brothers in religion."

NORODIN LUCMAN

When I returned to Manila the following day, I gave a lot of thought to how I would frame what I'd just experienced. To my surprise, I wound up posting a video called "I Smiled at War." I was not intending to be glib, and certainly not disrespectful, but it was my honest takeaway. Marawi had surprised me in more ways than one.

"If there is one thing I did not expect to do inside a war zone, it is smile," I began. "But even in the middle of a war, there are always reasons to smile. When I heard the bombs in the background and watched the smoke rising above the city, I walked half a mile down the street to a local university and saw hundreds of students waiting in line to enroll in classes. They were

VICTORY IN MARAWI

determined to get their education, even in the middle of a war zone. That made me smile.

"When I noticed that many of the students were women wearing niqabs—Muslim women pursuing an education—that made me smile. And though their faces were covered, I could see from the crinkles around their eyes that they were smiling, too.

"When I met with the president of the university, who told me that classes would begin the following week, we both smiled.

"Indeed, Marawi is a city almost entirely destroyed by war. But that's exactly why the stories of its people were important to share. In these war-torn regions, I am convinced that for every one ISIS-inspired fighter, there are ten thousand locals who just want to live their lives in peace."

The reaction to the video on Facebook was overwhelmingly positive, none more so than this comment from a young college student in Texas named Alana. "Thank you for this video," she wrote. "It has opened my eyes and changed the way I see people."

I left the Philippines on Day 512, headed for Japan. As of this writing, I have yet to return—but that doesn't mean I won't. Whatever it is about the country that has taken hold of me—the warm smiles, the easy friendships, the enduring sense of hope—it is now a part of who I am.

Fewer than eight weeks after my departure, the Battle of Marawi ended. The government won. The final death toll was 978 militants, 168 government forces, and 87 civilians. The city is being rebuilt again. Nor is now a war hero. The university is still open. And peace has prevailed.

"If ISIS came knocking at your door, what would you do?" In the people of Marawi, I had finally found my answer.

A MOUNTAIN OF LIFE VESTS LEFT BY SYRIAN REFUGEES IN LESBOS, GREECE

ONE GUY IS ALL IT TAKES

THE WORLD, DAY 736

The following incident happened to me while I was in a small city in the Mediterranean. The country isn't important.

I walked into a cell phone store with my colleague Agon and we stepped into the line. A man staggered in behind us and immediately approached me. He was obviously drunk, and Agon began filming us. We both sensed something was about to happen.

The man asked me where I was from.

"HE STAGGERED IN BEHIND AND IMMEDIATELY APPROACHED ME"

"Israel, Palestine, and the United States," I said. I tried to keep it as general as possible.

It didn't work—my answer set him off. He flew into a rage, ranting in fractured English and flailing his arms.

"Fuck you!" he screamed. "Yes, fuck you!" He started pacing the store like a caged tiger, striding up to me with each new condemnation and poking his finger in my face.

"This guy—Palestine!" he said directly into Agon's camera while gesturing to me. "Me, Libya. Gaddafi. *Gaddafi!*"

With each mention of Muammar Gaddafi's name, he stabbed at his own chest with his finger.

Then suddenly, he turned away from Agon, walked directly up to me, and cocked his arm back. His hand was balled into a fist.

Agon stopped filming, ready to join in the fight to defend his friend. I braced for the blow.

In the end, the guy chose not to punch me. Instead, he shouted a few more words of abuse and stumbled out the door. The police arrived moments later.

If it isn't obvious by now, the man was an immigrant, and he was exactly what people say they hate about immigrants: he represented danger. "Immigrants are going to hurt you," we're warned, "so you'd better be frightened of them."

And, yes, I admit it: when that man threatened me the way he did—his body coiled for attack, his face a picture of fury—I was frightened. And in that moment, I hated immigrants, too, which is really sad because I'm an immigrant myself.

And that, I think, is the biggest threat of all. It's not just this guy who's dangerous. It's me. It's us.

We look at him and say, "All of them are the same! Why do they threaten us like this? What did we ever do to them? Let's ban them all!" And the more we say this, the more we believe it. And the more we believe it, the more we dig in. And that insidious cycle continues, on and on, until finally it's not just the drunk in the cell phone store anymore, it's *all* immigrants who are the enemy—refugees, victims of war, people simply looking for a home.

"Immigrants are bad for our country!" our leaders tell us. "They take our jobs, they take our food, they take our lives. What's more, they're bad for our economy!"

IMMIGRANTS BUILT THE WORLD

Bad for our economy? Immigrants built America—and countless nations around the globe. And today, centuries later, even as the world heaps resentment on them—banning them, deporting them, breaking apart their families—they continue to provide the steam for our engines of economy.

They make the sandwich you grab on your lunch break.

They check you into the hotel room you book.

They pick the strawberry you eat.

They assemble the products you use.

They care for the children you love.

They invent the technology you use.

And, incidentally, they probably delivered the book you're holding.

Immigration is not a liberal or conservative issue. It's a human one—and I've personally witnessed the human toll exacted on immigrants in far too many places around the world.

I've seen the boats the Syrian refugees took to Greece to escape the killing in their homeland and the mountain of life vests they left on the shore.

I've seen the camps they lived in and photos of the families they lost.

I've met them online and in person, at home and in hiding, and what I can tell you is this: the only thing immigrants want is to live their lives.

And yet, there in that cell phone store in that small seaside city, my brain told me to be afraid of them—*all of them*—and I did as instructed. I became frightened of people who are just like me, and all because of one guy.

It always works like this. One guy ruins it for everybody—one guy in a store who had too much to drink and too little to hold on to. We focus our minds and our cameras and our hate on this one man, while ignoring whole populations around the world who are asking for nothing more than the freedom to exist in peace.

One guy is all it takes—because we let him.

I met Aleesha on a trip to Marawi, Philippines. I was in the country for one purpose: to see ISIS up-close. While there, I heard that three miles from the terror zone was a university that, despite the danger, was still operating. So I paid a visit. As I strolled the campus, a voice called out to me. "I enjoy watching your videos!" she said. And there was Aleesha. I was stunned—I'd never met a niqabi (a woman wearing a niqab—the traditional Muslim head and face covering) who wasn't shy. Lucky for us, no male companions were present to control what she said to me, so we talked. Aleesha told me that she was thirty-seven years old and not yet married, as one might have expected. She had her own job at the university and was surprisingly progressive ("I even have a gay friend!" she boasted). She said she preferred to wear a niqab because it helped her feel closer to God and made her life simpler. "I don't have to worry about wearing makeup just to impress others," she said. Like many Westerners, I find niqabs repressive. Aleesha disagreed. "People are fighting for my right," she said, "but they forget, this is also my right. It's my choice."

THE UNITED STATES THE $1 MICROSCOPE

Imagine you live in a poor country and want to drink water from the village creek, which may be contaminated with billions of tiny monsters—bacteria, viruses, and other creepy-crawly microbes. The only way to know for sure is by getting your hands on a $2,000 microscope, but that's not an option. What's the solution? Enter Manu Prakash and Jim Cybulski, a pair of brainiacs from Stanford University who invented a microscope capable of magnifying organisms up to two thousand times their actual size—and it costs just $1 to build. A new entry in the "frugal science" movement, which brings low-cost scien-

tific tools to the developing world, the Foldscope is made almost entirely of paper, and assembling it is downright fun. It's precut just like those tab-and-slot paper toys you constructed as a kid; and once you've folded it together, origami-style, you've got yourself a pocket-size window into a whole new universe—whether it's bacteria in your cow milk or a parasite in your crops. And because it's made of high-strength, plastic-coated paper, the Foldscope is practically indestructible—stamp on it, pour water on it, toss it off a building and the thing still works. Because of the Foldscope's insanely low $1 production cost, Manu and Jim were able to manufacture half a million of them and send them around the globe. "Just this morning," Manu told me, "I woke up to a picture on my phone of children in a village in India, exploring the microscopic world around them. This happens every day." Doctors in poor, remote areas are already using the Foldscope to protect their patients from diseases like rabies and malaria—and that, notes Jim, lies at the heart of the Foldscope mission: "It's important to make science affordable and accessible to everyone in the world," he says. "Now everyone can explore the microcosmos."

SEYCHELLES THE WORLD'S BIGGEST NUT!

In the eighteenth century, Praslin—the second largest island in the beautiful Seychelles archipelago—was used by seafaring pirates as a tropical safe haven where they could hide out and stash their stolen booty. Three centuries later, a different kind of booty resides on the island, and it's hiding in plain sight. I'm talking about the coco-de-mer, also known as the sea coconut, but most lovingly referred to as the "butt nut." The fruit of the island's native *Lodoicea maldivica* palm trees, butt nuts are seriously big—like, bigger than a human head—but they get their nickname because they're the size of an average human butt, and they look like one, too. Capable of growing as big as twenty inches in diameter, making them the largest seed in the plant kingdom, these babies are also heavy, tipping the scales at up to ninety pounds. Despite their worldwide fame, butt nuts grow in only two places on the planet—the islands of Praslin and Curieuse—and they're likely stuck there for good. That's because if one happens to fall off the tree into the ocean, it sinks rather than floats away. As for what a butt nut tastes like, no one really knows—they're so rare that it's illegal to eat them. But I took an immediate shine to the big fellas— because from now on, no one can call *me* the biggest nut in the world.

JAPAN $20,000 FOR FISH?!

I like to eat, and over the course of my Nas Daily travels, I sampled a lot of local cuisines—from the goat stew in Ethiopia to the fast food at Jollibee, the Philippines' homegrown answer to McDonald's. So naturally, on my visits to Japan, I went straight for the sushi—24-7. But after a while it wasn't enough just to eat good sushi; I had to see *why* it was so good. That's why I spent Day 686 at the Tsukiji Market in Tokyo, the largest fish and seafood wholesaler on the planet. Founded in 1935, the market is a sushi paradise—a complex that includes restaurants, kitchen supply stores, retail shops, and, of course, grocery stands where you can stock up for home. But I discovered the real

action when I slipped into Tsukiji's restricted "inner market," a busy trading floor where up to nine hundred licensed fishers and wholesalers congregate every morning to buy and sell their gorgeous bounty. These are people who have dedicated their entire lives to hauling in the best fish in the sea—the perfect color, the ideal fattiness, the incomparable freshness. And when they find that exquisite catch, someone will surely buy it for tens of thousands of dollars. Imagine that: a piece of fish that costs as much as a car. I was in awe watching these men and women working hard at something they loved, and when I walked out of that market, I was impressed and inspired. I was also really hungry.

CHINA THE VILLAGE OF SMALL FEET

Imagine if I gave you a pair of shoes that were a bit too small. You'd put them on, wince in pain, and remove them. Nobody likes tight shoes. But the women I met in a small rural village in Yunnan Province, China, had no choice in the matter. They were among the females of their era who were forced by custom to wear torturously tiny shoes. The practice was known as foot-binding, and it was a tradition that endured for ten centuries in China, only to be outlawed in 1912. The painful process was not intended as a punishment; rather, it was believed that diminutive feet signaled a young woman's refinement, beauty, status, and even sensuality. The cost, however, was steep. A young girl's foot would be tightly wrapped in strips of cloth—crushing the toes and clefting the arch—over time reducing the foot to a size that could fit into a four-inch-long silk "lotus shoe." Today, the dwindling population of foot-binding survivors—perhaps as few as five hundred of them—are scattered in villages throughout China, attracting tourists and journalists alike. The survivor I interviewed, a ninety-five-year-old grandmother, removed her shoe and showed me her foot, and, indeed, it was badly deformed. But as she spoke to me through an interpreter, she seemed strangely proud to have outlived a custom that was dangerous and unkind. I left the village feeling saddened—but also grateful that some traditions ultimately die.

PART 6
HUMANITY

Photo by Kevin Carter / Sygma / Sygma via Getty Images

WHY ARE WE BLIND TO AFRICA?

It is, perhaps, the most unsettling photograph the world has ever seen.

The year was 1993, and photographer Kevin Carter was in Ayod, in what is now South Sudan. At the time, the country was in the throes of a civil war, and Carter was among the photojournalists who had been invited by Operation Lifeline Sudan to chronicle the famine in the region. By then, nearly half of the children younger than five in the area were malnourished, and an estimated ten to thirteen adults died of starvation every day.

Carter had just come to a clearing in the brush outside a small village when he heard the crying. Then he saw the little boy—a toddler, emaciated—who had collapsed from hunger on his way to the feeding center. The child's small body was in a tight crouch, almost fetal, his forehead pressed to the sand. Carter had been advised by relief workers not to touch the famine victims on account of disease, so instead he shot a photograph. It was at that moment that a vulture swept into the frame and settled behind the child, its eyes trained on the little boy as if he were prey. Carter took another picture.

The *New York Times* published the photograph that same month, and within days it shot around the globe, ultimately appearing in newspapers and magazines and even on fund-raising posters for aid organizations. It eventually won the Pulitzer Prize, and it remains today an emblem of the suffering that exists in our world and a damning portrait of our neglect.

PROGRESS IN ETHIOPIA: A GROWING ECONOMY, THE RELEASE OF POLITICAL PRISONERS, AND NEW STRIDES IN GENDER EQUALITY

I remember first seeing the photo when I was a kid—I was only thirteen—and thinking that all of Africa was like that. Poverty. Danger. Death. And if I'm going to be completely honest, I carried those same presumptions into adulthood.

But I don't blame myself entirely. This is the picture that is commonly painted of Africa—the forgotten continent, a place of tribal wars and starvation, dictatorships and terrorism. And yet what's often overlooked about Africa is its startling statistics. At 11.7 million square miles, it is the second largest continent on the planet, home to one billion people who speak more than fifteen hundred different languages, and the very birthplace of human civilization.

When I began Nas Daily, I was realistic enough to know that I was ignorant about Africa, and I was determined to change that. And by the time I'd visited my third and fourth country there, I began to wonder why so little is written about its progress.

Take Ethiopia, whose one hundred million citizens make it the second most populated country on the continent (after Nigeria). On paper, Ethiopia is poor, with 24 percent of its people living below the poverty line. That's probably what you've read in your newspaper, and it's certainly what you've seen on the nightly news. But did you also know that in 2018, the poverty rate was nearly half of what it had been just twenty years earlier? Or that thanks to the government's investment in public infrastructure and industrial parks, the Ethiopian economy was increasing by 10 percent every year, making it one of the fastest-growing economies on the planet?

This great acceleration forward isn't limited to just money matters. It's about the country's leadership, too. In February 2018, nearly two years after my visit to Ethiopia with Nas Daily, the nation's prime minister stepped down from power—the first leader in the country's modern history to do so—making way for a successor who promised reform. That reinvention happened. Old-style authoritarianism was abolished, democracy began thriving, government corruption plummeted, political prisoners were released, exiled dissidents were invited home, and the twenty-year conflict with neighboring Eritrea at long last ended.

And, oh yes, the prime minister installed a cabinet that was 50 percent female, while the nation's parliament elected a woman president for the first time in the country's history. Why wasn't that on the front pages?

I just don't get it. When reform began blooming in Saudi Arabia, the whole world cheered, especially when women were finally permitted to drive. But when steps are taken toward gender equality in an African country, where is the cheering? An entire nation transforms itself dramatically—for the better—in just six months, and nobody wants to talk about it. This is real tangible change, and it should be noticed, supported, and held up as an example for other emerging nations.

And then there are the people of Ethiopia, whose good hearts and deeply held aspirations I've never forgotten. Inside those poor farm villages, right next to the desolation and dried-up lakes, I met scores of Ethiopians who invited me into their homes, prepared meals for me, and told me, time and again, that they wanted the same life as mine—and yours. These were not the grass-skirted, war-painted natives I saw in my schoolbooks and in the pages of *National Geographic*. They weren't the warlords in military fatigues and aviator sunglasses who regularly pop up in Hollywood action films. These were real live people who just wanted a better life.

"What do you want to do when you grow up?" I asked a young man in a remote village in Harar, and he couldn't have answered me faster.

"I'm going to go to Harvard University," he told me.

And it's not only Ethiopia that's putting muscle behind its dreams. When I visited Nigeria on Day 73, I met a group of young entrepreneurs in Lagos who were hiring the best and brightest minds in the country and turning

them into computer coders and engineers, the hope being that they will help Nigeria become a world leader in global technology. Their work was so impressive that Facebook titan Mark Zuckerberg had already invested $24 million in them to train one hundred thousand young techies within the next decade. You don't have to be a global economist to know that nobody forks over that kind of dough to a project unless it has real promise.

Certainly Africa continues to face challenges, and I saw those up-close, too. When I visited the tiny southern nation of Swaziland on Day 604, I was knocked sideways by the country's stunning wildlife reserves and its insane cultural history (including a reigning king who has fifteen wives and twenty-three children). But I was also heartbroken to learn that one in four Swazis is infected with HIV, seven in ten live in poverty, and the average life expectancy in the country has dipped to as low as forty-nine years—one of the shortest life spans in the world.

Likewise Madagascar, where half a century of violent dictatorships and military coups have taken their toll: nearly 80 percent of its people live below the poverty line. I had traveled there inspired by its sheer beauty; I left sobered by its disheartening numbers.

And yet, it is critical to remember that these dour statistics are rapidly improving and that countries like Ethiopia have begun holding high a beacon to light the path forward for her sister nations.

It is my hope that the rest of the world can learn from Ethiopia, too. Perhaps then we can look at that searing photograph of the starving child in Sudan and not just mourn Africa's past, but grow excited for its future.

Note: Subsequent research into Kevin Carter's photograph revealed that the child ultimately survived, but died fourteen years later from malarial fever. The year after Carter shot the historic photo, he took his own life. In a note he left behind, he wrote, "I am haunted by the vivid memories of killings & corpses & anger & pain."

WHAT I LEARNED
FROM A FROG

Let's say you want to boil a frog. You put a pot of water on the stove, crank up the heat, and when it reaches a boil you place the frog inside of it. But, smart fellow that he is, the frog will immediately jump out of the water because it's too hot. This is a fact.

So now you have to go to Plan B. Instead of boiling the water first, you place the frog in warm water. He will stay there because he'll just think he's taking a nice bath. Then, slowly but surely, you turn up the heat. The frog will not notice this temperature change because it's small and incremental. Soon bubbles will appear, but the frog still won't complain—he'll just think he's now in a bubble bath.

But when the water reaches 212 degrees, it will boil and the frog will be . . . dead. Mission accomplished.

Now, if this is how you can boil a frog to death, what does that tell you about nature? It tells you that frogs and humans stay away from the big, dangerous things. Frogs stay away from boiling water because they can get hurt. Humans stay away from hurricanes (and gunfire and railroad tracks and shopping malls the day after Thanksgiving, etc.) because they can get hurt, too.

But here's the catch: just like frogs, humans fail to notice the small things. The small changes in someone's behavior. The small leak under the kitchen sink. The small pivot in a political campaign. The small dip in the economy. Or even the tiny, 1.8-degree rise in global temperatures—which on paper seems like nothing, but up in glacier country can mean the beginning of the end.

Small stuff adds up. We see this all around us—like with rent. Your rent goes up $10 or $15 every couple of months, and it's no big deal—until a few years down the line, when you find yourself looking at your monthly rent bill and mumbling, "Why the heck am I paying so much to live in a box? How did I get here?!"

And it's not just about numbers. It can be much more personal—like a relationship. Abusive relationships start small. One nasty word here, one heated argument there, then maybe a small, one-off act of violence, like a shove or a smack.

"Oh, he's just tired and grumpy from work," she'll say, applying ice to her swollen eye.

"Oh, she just had an argument with her mother and she's upset," he'll say, putting a bandage on his chin.

And before you know it, three years have passed and something very, very bad has happened. Something that you "didn't see coming."

So this is what the boiling frog experiment has taught me—that everything around us is changing slowly but surely, and it's up to us to recognize the negative changes and fix them before it's too late.

And now for a confession: I lied about the frog—that story is just an old myth. In reality, a frog *will* notice the incremental temperature change in the water. He is well aware of his surroundings, and when things get too hot, he'll jump out of the pot. I mean, the guy's not an idiot.

So the real question is, if frogs can notice small changes and act on them, then why can't humans?

THE MEXICALI DESERT

THE MEXICO YOU
NEVER SEE

MEXICO, DAY 526

"Stereotypes fall in the face of humanity," the writer Anna Quindlen once wrote. "We human beings are best understood one at a time."

I couldn't agree more, especially given that in my twenty-seven years, I've been labeled and typecast in more ways than any single human being should have to tolerate: Crazy Arab. Godless Palestinian. Terrorist. Tech nerd. Harvard elitist. Fame-seeker.

By Day 526, my Nas Daily viewers were well aware that I think stereotypes suck, so it must have come as a surprise to them that I would celebrate my first full day in Mexico City by cramming my Facebook video with every predictable south-of-the-border trope I could think of:

Me waving a Mexican flag, standing in front of a mariachi band as it blasted out a lively rendition of "El Jarabe Tapatío" (Google it—trust me, you've heard it).

Alyne dancing alongside me, cradling a tiny stuffed *toro*.

Some guy eating a taco; another dude doing tequila shots.

A blindfolded white woman in a Mexican shirt—the kind you buy in a souvenir shop—swatting the shit out of a piñata.

¡Viva la México!

No, I hadn't gone insane. In fact, the whole reason I'd come to Mexico was to illustrate the absurdity of stereotypes. The Mexico we see on the nightly news—a country filled with drug-dealing, border-jumping, shotgun-toting *bandoleros*—is just as shallow and empty as a papier-mâché donkey, *without* the candy inside. I wanted to do just the opposite and explore the beautiful cradle of civilization that Mexico really is. I was on a mission.

Starting the next day, I began to uncover the Mexico that I rarely see on the news, and to do that, I stepped up to the stereotypes that the media likes to traffic in when they talk about the country.

Stereotype: Mexico doesn't contribute to the global culture.

Wrong. Mexico has made countless contributions, large and small, to our lives—it's just that we don't know about them. From the Caesar salad on your plate to the birth control pill in your medicine chest, humankind wouldn't be humankind without a serious Mexican assist.

The inventions are endless. That color television in your living room, that Cuervo in your liquor cabinet, that guac you scarf down at Chipotle—all of them bear the unmistakable insignia of the ol' red-white-and-green. Even that "Swiss" chocolate bar in your fridge comes to us originally not from Switzerland or Belgium, but from the ancient Mayans, who first whipped up chocolate—aka "the food of the gods"—in the forests of the Yucatán Peninsula three thousand years ago.

"Made in Mexico," it turns out, is more accurate than you might think.

¡VIVA LA MÉXICO!

Stereotype: Mexicans prefer to come to the United States illegally because there is no opportunity for work in their own country.

I won't get political here—let's just say that there's been a lot of talk in recent years about the need to build a great big wall on America's southern border to keep Mexicans and other brown people out. Undocumented immigration is a real problem at the border—that's undeniable—and there are countless reasons why these men and women and children risk their lives every day to attempt that illegal crossing. But the suggestion that there's no work to be found in their homelands is patently wrong.

On Day 531, I traveled to Mexicali, the capital of the Mexican state of Baja California and its second largest city (after Tijuana). My goal was to see for myself the infamous wall that stands there and to explore what life is like on the Mexican side of it. The first thing I did was launch my drone, which sent me back the whole story. On one side of the wall—the Mexican side—was a crowded grid of streets that bore a striking resemblance to the congested neighborhoods of South Central Los Angeles. On the American side were acres upon acres of farmland, and not a house or automobile in sight. I couldn't help but notice how, from the air, at least, the grass is literally greener on the other side of the fence.

I then took a trip out to the portion of the desert where most illegal crossings are attempted. The sheer expanse of the area—and the oppressive heat—made me realize just how hard these escapes into the United States are. At one point, I stumbled upon a lone grave marker on a patch of sand—a simple white cross bearing the name of a person who didn't make it—and that one sight made everything chillingly real.

And yet when I ventured into a few of the farm communities in Mexicali, I saw the story that American newspapers don't often tell. It's the story of opportunity.

Here were Mexicans who didn't make it to the United States for whatever reason—some had gotten caught and sent back, others had not even tried—but here's the kicker: they found jobs in Mexico instead. Yes, opportunity exists on the southern side of the border, where, thanks to government subsidies and access to fresh running water, men and women are hard at work around the clock, locals and immigrants alike.

I spent the day among this workforce and was blown away by their enterprising spirit. I saw teams of farmers harvesting newly grown crops while

WORKING AT THE MEXICAN BORDER

others planted palm trees. I met Americans who had moved to Mexico to start their own businesses, with the hopes of making good money and having fun in the Mexican sun. I spoke with locals who were simply grateful to have a job.

As one Mexican farmer told me with a weary smile as he stacked huge crates of dates, "This is my gold mine."

Stereotype: Mexicans don't care about their country.

I can't remember what I'd originally intended to shoot on September 19, 2017. All I know is that at 1:14 p.m. that day everything changed.

"Hi," my video began that night. "Today a 7.1 magnitude earthquake hit Mexico City—one of the strongest in the city's history. My friends, my girlfriend, and I are all safe. But I'm taking the first flight back to Mexico City because many people there are in real danger. Entire buildings have collapsed, 150 people have died—including schoolchildren—and many more are still trapped. This is a real disaster."

Looking back at that day's video, I'm struck by how rattled I was. My eyes are bloodshot and my voice is raspy, either from screaming or exhaustion. As it turns out, the numbers got much worse in the ensuing hours. The quake had struck thirty-five miles south of the city of Puebla, sending powerful shock waves into the region. In all, an estimated 370 people were killed—two-thirds of them in Mexico City—and more than 6,000 were injured.

I spent the next day roaming Mexico City, capturing footage of the damage wreaked by the quake, as well as the relief effort that was underway to find those who were still trapped or missing. Steam shovels clawed at giant hills of stone and rubble, searching for signs of life; crushed cars lined the streets; the sounds of work crews and sirens filled the air, occasionally punctured by the shrieks of bystanders when another building fell. And, as always, the human suffering was the most painful to witness.

MEXICO CITY EARTHQUAKE, SEPTEMBER 2017

"I think my brother is in there," a man wearing a surgical mask told me weakly, pointing to the smoky heap of steel and concrete behind him. His voice trailed off. He appeared to be in shock.

And yet something else was going on that day in Mexico City, and it was stronger than any earthquake could ever be. It was humanity. Within just hours of those first terrifying tremors, the city had turned from a place of destruction into a haven of hope. Tents popped up on sidewalks, providing shelter for those whose homes had been destroyed. Pedestrians formed bucket brigades across the streets, passing supplies and bottles of water to the rescuers who were excavating the piles of debris. One woman parked her car alongside a worksite and set up a buffet table covered with chicken, rice, and beans—like a mobile restaurant—to feed the emergency responders. And locals everywhere cruised the boulevards in their cars, providing free taxi service to anyone who needed a lift.

When I posted the video on Facebook that evening, the outpouring of support from thousands of my viewers was just as potent as what I'd witnessed on the streets. I was especially moved by comments from Mexicans themselves.

"Now you are seeing what we Mexicans are made of," wrote one. "We are stronger when we work together. I am so proud of my people!"

I'm going to be honest. I had arrived in Mexico knowing nothing about the country, and I wasn't really looking forward to it. From what I'd read in the papers, it was a place of danger and despair. But I had gone there to grow—and that is exactly what happened. I left Mexico at the end of two weeks changed by what I'd seen. Whether it was a borderland farmer rising above angry politics to take pride in his work, or a collective people joining together for a few days to rescue their city in its most harrowing moment of crisis, this was a country that had smashed my preconceived perceptions like the flimsiest of piñatas and, in the process, opened my eyes to the beauty of Mexicans.

¡Viva la México!

FORGIVENESS, JUSTICE, AND THE FUTURE

RWANDA, DAY 398

"By the time you finish watching this video, seven people would have died. Seven. That was the case only twenty-three years ago here in Rwanda, where more than one million perished in just one hundred days. While the entire world stood by, Rwanda died."

THE PRISTINE STREETS OF KIGALI, RWANDA

With those words I began my journey through a country that was completely off my radar. In fact, I was very forthcoming about this blind spot when I first arrived in Rwanda in May 2017.

"Oh, my God," I told viewers in my first video from the tiny subtropical nation, which lies in the Great Lakes region of Central Africa. "I just woke up jet-lagged in a country I know nothing about. Welcome to Rwanda!"

My goal in this exceptionally pretty country was to get to know it better through its people. And if you're going to learn about the people of Rwanda, you need to understand the most tragic event in their nation's history: the genocide against the Tutsi people in 1994.

In 1990, a civil war erupted in Rwanda. At the center of the conflict were the Hutu and the Tutsi, rival ethnic groups that had been at each other's throats since Rwanda had first won its independence from Belgium nearly thirty years earlier.

The war was between the Hutu majority-rule government and the Rwandan Patriotic Front, which was largely composed of Tutsi refugees who had been forced out of the country decades earlier and had now returned, armed and angry.

Guerrilla violence between the two factions dominated the early years of the war, which was then followed by a tentative peace accord. But on April 6, 1994, an airplane carrying the Hutu president was shot down, killing him and the president of neighboring Burundi. No one knew who had ordered or conducted the assassination, but that didn't slow the retaliation. The next day—and for the ensuing ninety-nine days—the Hutu carried out mass exterminations,

REMEMBERING THE RWANDAN GENOCIDE

during which an estimated one million Rwandans died, a staggering annihilation that obliterated approximately 80 percent of the entire Tutsi population.

The genocide was as brutal as it was brisk. Militias, soldiers, and police methodically executed key Tutsi leaders and their followers; barricades were thrown up, checkpoints established, IDs issued. And the hit squads did not discriminate for age or gender: men, women, and children were all ruthlessly cut down; husbands killed their own wives because of their ethnicity. Government forces also recruited Hutu civilians to rape, maim, and slaughter their Tutsi neighbors and destroy their homes—and no weapon was off-limits. Machetes and clubs played a large part of the bloody massacre.

The world watched in horror as the butchery continued, and both the United States and the United Nations were widely condemned for sitting on their hands. The carnage finally came to an end on July 4, when the Rwandan Patriotic Front captured the capital city of Kigali and seized control of the government, driving two million Rwandans—most of them Hutu—into neighboring countries.

Today, the three-month bloodletting is commemorated with two public holidays in Rwanda—one that mourns the genocide of 1994, and the other that celebrates the country's liberation that followed.

But it is the people of Rwanda—those who witnessed and survived the genocide—who gave me the greatest insight into the inhumanity of those dark days, and the inspiring humanity that arose from it.

On my third day in Kigali, I was introduced to a woman named Ernestine, whose recollections of the genocide were chilling. If you saw Ernestine on the street, you might not give her a second glance. A woman of average height with short-cropped hair and a pleasant smile, she wore thick black glasses that give her the air of a university professor. But if you looked a bit more closely, you'd see the five-inch scar on her neck. That scar tells her story.

Ernestine took me back to that day in 1994 when Hutu soldiers stormed her village. She and her family hid out in a church, she told me, desperately praying that they would not become the latest statistic in the tragedy that was wrecking their country. Sadly, those prayers weren't answered, as all six of Ernestine's family members were killed in front of her.

Ernestine barely had time to register the atrocity that was taking place. Amid the violence, she was viciously assaulted—a machete to the neck—and her hands were tied behind her back. She was then thrown into the river and left to die.

Amazingly, after the soldiers ran from the village, Ernestine found her way back to shore, surviving what should have been certain death. But if that unlikely turn of events was miraculous—and it was—what she told me next left me speechless. After the country was liberated and Ernestine tried to reassemble her life, she made peace with the soldiers who had slain her family and tried to kill her.

She introduced me to one of them. His name was Patrick, and he was among those who tore into her village and shot up her church on that awful day. Following the country's liberation, he pled guilty to the crime of genocide before the tribunal that had been established in Rwanda, and he served time in jail. Upon his release, he sought forgiveness from his victims as part of his personal redemption. Despite her trauma, Ernestine granted Patrick that forgiveness. She even invited him to her wedding.

In the thousand days that I traveled the world for Nas Daily, there were only a handful of times that I was left both humbled and inspired by what I'd witnessed. This was one of those times. Watching Ernestine and Patrick through my camera's viewfinder—sitting on a couch, his arm draped behind her, talking and laughing like old friends—convinced me that forgiveness is more powerful than justice.

Growing up in the Middle East, I became inured to the rhetoric of "justice." Israelis and Palestinians called for justice all the time. Justice for the massacres of seventy years ago. Justice for those who were wronged on both sides. And these calls intensified over the years, especially on the Palestinian side. It began to feel like a better future for the country depended entirely on whether or not justice was served.

This simplified notion of justice doesn't exist only in embattled countries. It's big in Hollywood, too. Think about how many movies you've seen in which justice is romanticized. *Justice is sought. Justice is fought for. Justice is served!*

The problem is, justice is impossible to achieve. And if my time in Rwanda taught me anything, it's that sometimes working for the future of a country is more important than dwelling on reparations for the past. Ernestine did not serve her family's killer justice. She served him forgiveness—and that is a lot more powerful.

FORGIVING HER FAMILY'S MURDERER

Ernestine wasn't alone in her mercy. In the years following the Rwandan genocide, millions of survivors forgave their families' killers as part of the country's National Unity and Reconciliation process, which sought to heal the nation's wounds in hopes of building a better nation. Fast-forward twenty-five years, and Rwanda—which is often referred to as "the Heart of Africa"—is a shining reflection of those efforts. During my time inside the country, I found ample evidence of that amazing growth.

I shot footage of the astonishingly pristine streets of Kigali—so clean and safe you could sleep on them.

I reported on the rise of women in the country, thanks in part to its Ministry of Gender and Family Promotion, a government agency that ensures gender equality and women's empowerment in Rwanda's national policies.

And I attended the country's annual Transform Africa summit in Kigali, where I was blown away by the bottomless talent pool of young people, united under the flag of Rwanda, who are working hard to build technology companies that will steer the country to an even brighter future.

In October 2018, the president of Rwanda, Paul Kagame, spoke to Brandon Stanton, the creator of *Humans of New York*, and once again retraced his nation's journey back from the brink of destruction. The eloquence of Kagame's words and the depth of his humanity truly moved me.

"How do you pursue justice when the crime is so great?" Kagame asked. "You can't lose one million people in one hundred days without an equal number of perpetrators. But we also can't imprison an entire nation. So forgiveness was the only path forward. Survivors were asked to forgive and forget.

"Rwanda's future was more important than justice. It was a huge burden to place on the survivors, but I don't know what to ask the perpetrators. 'Sorry' won't bring back any lives. Only forgiveness can heal this nation. The burden rests with the survivors because they are the only ones with something to give."

I spent seven days in Rwanda, and what I took with me when I left—and still carry with me today—was the enduring and hopeful message of the Rwandans themselves. "If the people of Rwanda can forgive the person who took away the lives of their families," I told viewers, "then we can forgive anyone."

When Mpho Makutu was just ten years old and living in rural South Africa, he liked to tinker, building toy cars from tin cans and whatever spare electrical parts he found around the house. This didn't please his father, especially when Mpho starting ripping apart Dad's stereo system. The boy was punished but that didn't stop him. When I first met Mpho (then twenty and a mechanical engineering student), he was seated on a sidewalk bench in Soweto—South Africa's largest township—operating a funky-looking, five-foot robot made entirely from garbage. This was his low-tech way of busking: showing off the contraption that he'd cobbled together from discarded cardboard, Coke cans, wire hangers, a machine drill, and an old elevator battery, and hoping passersby would pony up some spare change for the entertainment. It looked like a mini-construction site crane, which Mpho operated with seven electric levers he built. It didn't do a whole lot either—it made a few herky-jerky turns, and then the crane picked up objects—but, hey, *he'd built it from trash*! Mpho's dream is to one day enter the high-stakes world of robotics—to have his own workshop and provide jobs for his fellow citizens. If he were living in California, I thought, he already would have been snapped up by Google or Apple for his talent and dedication. But for now, Mpho seemed content doing his apprenticeship on the sidewalk of a South African township, waiting to be recognized.

THE PHILIPPINES **A HUGE CHANGE**

Born into wealth and blessed with ambition, Ian King had everything a guy could want: great looks, a vibrant personality, a supermodel-wife, and even moderate fame in the Philippines as a championship race-car driver. But Ian had a secret. Ian wanted to be Angie. It was a dream that had been tucked inside ever since Ian was a child—that is, until Ian's father died. "I couldn't go on living like that any longer," Ian told me. "Life is too short not to be happy." So after many sleepless nights and a couple deep breaths, Ian transitioned to Angelina Mead King, and she's never looked back. She broke the news to friends and family on her private Instagram account, changing her username from "Hail to the King" to "Hail to the Queen." Instagram mistakenly turned the private post public, and Angie braced for the worst, expecting disgust, outrage, and rejection. To the contrary: nearly all of her followers ("99 percent!" she said) greeted her with encouragement, support, and love. Angie's inspiring story continues to be one of hope for so many people who struggle with gender identity. At age thirty-seven, Angie remains happily married to her wife, Joey, and continues to design, build, and race cars. She also has seventeen tattoos, manages hotels on the side, and knows how to fly a helicopter. If she decides to change her name again, I'd propose "Wonder Woman."

SINGAPORE HE DOESN'T BUY ANYTHING!

When I first met Daniel Tay, *Crazy Rich Asians* had just landed in movie theaters around the world. But Daniel, a thirty-nine-year-old former financial planner in Singapore, gave me a whole new spin on the subject of money. Daniel is what people call a "freegan," a practitioner of an emerging lifestyle based on "limited participation in the conventional economy and minimal consumption of resources," as one freegan website puts it. In other words, the guy has a lot of money but doesn't spend any of it. Instead of paying for food, Daniel gets it for free. In restaurants, he scarfs down whatever diners have left on their plates; on the street, he collects unsold produce from sidewalk fruit and vegetable vendors; at home, he's happy to bag up the week-old groceries his neighbors were about to toss. And like many freegans, Daniel is an expert dumpster diver.

Among the goodies he's scavenged during his midnight runs: a watch, a backpack, clothes, shampoo, umbrellas, speakers, a PlayStation, and even a refrigerator. "One person's trash is another person's treasure!" Daniel likes to say. I confess I was pretty impressed with Daniel's fiscal strategy. Here's a guy with $150,000 in savings who realized that the only sure way to make that money last forever is never to spend a cent of it. *Ka-ching!*

THE UNITED STATES A HOME FOR THE HOUSELESS

They don't call themselves "homeless"—they prefer "houseless"—yet they've come to define the word *community*. In 2007, a band of disadvantaged Hawaiians began setting up camp in a patch of woods next to the state-owned Waianae Small Boat Harbor, thirty miles northwest of Honolulu. Down on their luck but not in their spirit, they soon turned their pop-up refuge into a little tent city called Pu'uhonua o Waianae (population 270). Their mission was twofold: to dispel the myth that all homeless people are impoverished, dangerous substance abusers; and to provide support and shelter for one another as they looked to improve their lives.

Residency in the village has its rules: you may not make noise after 8:00 p.m.; you may not steal or do drugs; and you must keep your dog leashed. "We have a zero-tolerance policy," their leader told me, "and if you break the rules, you're out." The village also requires residents—60 percent of whom have jobs—to put in eight hours each month of community service, a mandate that has led to the construction of additional camp facilities, including a small park for the kids, an outdoor gym, a compact vegetable farm, and a little petting zoo. Also, all residents must learn American Sign Language. Why? Because among the villagers is a deaf child, and they want him to feel included. When I visited Pu'uhonua o Waianae, the villagers were in a celebratory mood. Word of their efforts had gone viral, and donations had begun streaming in, putting them closer to the $1.5 million it will cost them to buy their own land. And what will they do with that land once they sign the deed? Build homes on it.

NEW ZEALAND TOUCH NOSES WITH SOMEONE

When I first arrived in New Zealand—all the way down there at the bottom of the world—I expected to see only white people because, as a former British colony, the country remains ethnically European. But when I drove to the township of Taupo in the northern part of the country, I had the privilege of meeting the Māori, New Zealand's indigenous peoples whose ancestors first arrived on its shores from Polynesia—by canoe—four hundred years before the Europeans. Although today the Māori make up barely 15 percent of the population, they still refer to New Zealand by the name their people originally gave it, Aotearoa—which means "land of the long, white cloud"—and they continue to identify fiercely as Māori through their unique culture. Their tools and weapons are shaped like the bodies of their ancestors; and they decorate their skin with tattoos that represent the things they hold dear, such as family and nutrition and protection. To them, being Māori is not defined by the color of their skin but instead by their heritage, language, and genealogy. I felt an immediate bond with these remarkable people because I, too, have felt marginalized in my own homeland; so I took inspiration from the way the Māori have held faithfully to their culture over the centuries. I will never forget the way I was greeted by the first Māori elder I met in Taupo. According to custom, he approached me, closed his eyes, and pressed his nose to mine, because, in the Māori culture, you only know a person if you share a breath with him. More than anything, that's what makes a Māori Māori.

PART 7
LOOKING FORWARD

ALWAYS A STEP AHEAD

"I hate Singapore."

With those three words I began my two-and-a-half-week return trip to the tiny, pretty island-nation that sits elegantly at the bottom of the Malay Peninsula.

Don't get me wrong. I like pretty, shiny things. So why did I say I hate Singapore? Because I'm jealous of it.

Originally founded in 1819 as a trading post of the British East India Company, Singapore ultimately became a jewel in the crown of the British Raj—that sprawling collection of territories in the Indian subcontinent that the Brits scooped up and colonized in order to compete with Dutch merchants. But in 1963, Singapore rebelled against its Brit occupiers, teaming up with a handful of its colonized siblings to form what is now called Malaysia. Then two years later, after heated political and economic in-fighting, Singapore was expelled from Malaysia by the country's parliament, and ultimately gained its independence as a sovereign state, beginning its half-century rise to become what I consider the very model of a modern, major nation.

If you haven't been to Singapore, you need only look at photos to see that something unusually wonderful is going on there.

Its city skylines are dominated by gleaming towers and sky bridges that make you feel as if you've been transported to a future world.

Its compact landscape is graced with pristine parks and immaculate highways and a dazzling seaport that, when lit at night with every color in the spectrum, surely makes the Disneyland gang turn neon green with envy.

Its shopping malls could be their own country.

Yet while all this metropolitan eye candy was catnip for my drone, what made—and makes—Singapore so special to me is the powerful Asian melting pot it has become. It's the only place on the planet where people from three crazily diverse cultures—Chinese, Malaysian, and Indian—came together on a compact island, snapped up their independence, and built a high-tech, picture-perfect, kick-ass paradise.

But don't just take my word for it—do your own Google search. Wikipedia, for instance, credits Singapore as being a global hub for education, entertainment,

SINGAPORE, BY DAY AND NIGHT

finance, health care, innovation, manufacturing, technology, tourism, trade, and transport. It has also been lauded as the world's "most technology-ready nation," "smartest city," and "safest country."

And, from my own personal experience, Singapore is also one of the few places I've visited where, instead of getting hassled at the airport, I instantly felt welcomed. Culture and race and heritage are celebrated in Singapore, not used against you. As a Muslim Arab, I find that very refreshing.

Is Singapore a little uptight about its rules? Yes, it is. Selling chewing gum is still illegal in the country, as is drunk and disorderly conduct, using a fake ID, littering, not flushing the toilet after you pee, and being disrespectful to public servants. And then there was that nasty little international incident in 1994 when an eighteen-year-old American was sentenced to "six strokes of the cane" (i.e., a public whupping) after pleading guilty to vandalizing cars and stealing road signs. Ouch.

Still, Singapore's report card is so glowing that when I arrived there on Day 865—my second time in the country with Nas Daily—I decided to investigate this very pursuit of perfection.

The first sign came before I'd even left the airport. Weighing in at five stories and five square miles, Changi Airport is less an international hub for sixty-two million annual travelers than it is an epic playground. Got some time to kill after you've checked in? Then feel free to meander among the airport's endless array of amenities, which include a full-service swimming pool, a movie theater, a museum, sunflower and butterfly gardens, an activity center (complete with a massive orange climbing cage and a giant slide), a barbershop, self-flushing toilets, comfy sleeping lounges (with real, hotel-size beds), an endless array of restaurants (from international cuisine to Yankee-style Krispy Kreme), and what has to be a zillion USB docking stations.

Once Alyne and I settled in at our hotel—a typical mid-priced joint that in any other nation would be deemed five-star luxury for its swankiness—we began exploring the many secrets to Singaporean success. We started by paying a visit to a little resort island on the southern coast that was the picture of romance—lush, green fields dotted with flowers; smooth, white beaches lined with palms; secluded little parks—and was perfect for an afternoon picnic.

Now what if I told you that this sweet sanctuary is mostly a landfill? It's true—the lovely little island of Semakau is where Singapore carts its trash. Authorities collect the rubbish on the main island, burn it (carefully filtering

FUN AT CHANGI AIRPORT: FROM SWIMMING AND CLIMBING TO BUTTERFLIES AND FLOWERS

ROMANCE IN A LANDFILL

the smoke for any pollutants), gather the ashes, dump them into big, yellow trucks, and then ship them to this landscaped islet where they're poured into the still waters of a discreetly and ingeniously engineered containment pool. The garbage doesn't stink, the environment is unharmed, the wildlife still roam free, and the sea coral still thrives. Indeed, the landfill is so insanely sanitary that thirty yards away from the dump site is a fish farm whose finned inhabitants are 100 percent safe to eat—and it's all so scenic that newly engaged couples actually come to Semakau to take their wedding photos.

This same conscientiousness applies to the way Singapore disposes of unwanted food. On Day 873, I opened my video sitting among crates of produce that, at first glance, seemed perfectly fine. Sure, the celery was a bit limp, the bananas were slightly bruised, and the red peppers had lost a bit of their shine. But for someone in need, the food was perfectly healthy—a feast, even.

"But believe it or not, all of this is going into the garbage," I said. "It's not because these fruits and vegetables aren't good to eat—but because they're not good looking enough to sell."

It's a sad but true fact—food waste is a huge problem around the world. In the United States alone, 40 percent of food goes unsold, often because it has small imperfections or its color is slightly off; and for businesses, it's easier to throw away than to donate to the needy.

But in Singapore, food donation centers work tirelessly to rescue and distribute the eight hundred thousand tons of food that go to waste in the country every year. All by itself, Food Bank Singapore works with more than two hundred charity organizations eager to take that soft melon or pale tomato off the hands of grocers and redistribute them to people who don't care what they look like. I spent a single day with one of these vital organizations—SG Food Rescue—and we collected one and a half tons of produce.

"Food waste will not stop unless we change how we *look* at food," I reminded my viewers, "because just like humans, it's what's inside that matters, not the outside."

Recycling in Singapore doesn't stop at food; government agencies are equally dogged about the country's water. For example, if you had told me that one day I'd drink a nice cool bottle of pee, I would have said you were out of your mind. But the bottle of water I was drinking, every sip of it, was conceivably once in a toilet.

Before you throw up, hear me out. As strange as it seems for a nation floating in the Pacific, Singapore has always suffered a shortage of fresh water. The good stuff piped in from Malaysia makes up only about 30 percent of its supply, and another 30 percent comes from the island's own reservoirs. But building additional reservoirs is tough for a nation so tiny—especially one that likes to raise stunning towers on every available inch of land.

WATER PURIFICATION PLANT

So in 2003, Singapore joined the growing global trend of turning sewage and wastewater into the fresh drinkable stuff, and now the country pumps out twenty million gallons of what it calls NEWater every day.

I visited one of Singapore's four purification plants and saw the process with my own eyes. Inside a cavernous warehouse filled with tanks and turbines and a complex network of brightly painted turquoise pipes, workers in uniformed waistcoats and white safety helmets sanitize every single molecule of the dirty water until it's cleaner and more sparkling than the stuff you buy in bottles. In order to be ruled safe, the water is tested 150,000 times. This is by no means an easy process, and it's one more example of how Singapore goes that extra yard to do things right.

For the remainder of my time in Singapore, I investigated the other ways—large and small—that the country consistently earns gold stars. Its passport, for instance, is the second strongest in the world (after Japan), permitting visa-free access to 189 countries. That's because Singapore is not interested in invading or taking over other lands. All it wants is to be friends with its global neighbors, which makes life better for its citizens.

Its traffic is the least road-ragey I've ever seen, largely because of a strictly enforced limit to how many cars can be on the road at one time and a well-organized public transportation system. Singaporeans also pay careful attention to parking etiquette, never straying over the painted lines in lots and always pulling into their parking spots tail-first to save a little space.

And, of course, the people of Singapore themselves could not be kinder or more welcoming. The world can learn a lot from them. During my stay, I began calling it "an almost perfect country," because, marvelous as the place is, it's still got its share of problems. Contrary to the "crazy rich Asian" stereotype, Singapore—like most places on earth—struggles with income inequality and high prices. The average Singaporean makes just enough money to get by; the people who build those magnificent towers (that tourists like me stay in) are typically foreign workers who earn just $1.90 an hour; and 42 percent of the country's elderly can't afford to retire.

But what differentiates Singapore from the rest of the global pack is that it began a self-improvement campaign more than half a century ago and it has never slowed down.

PARKING IN SINGAPORE

Here's a place roughly the size of Austin, Texas, where 5.6 million people of varying cultures practically live on top of each other, and yet rather than hate one another for their differences, they've decided to live in harmony.

Here's a place where parents are more concerned with giving their children an education than giving them weapons.

Here's a place that might be a little obsessive about its rules and regulations but holds fast to its number-one rule of tolerance and acceptance.

Here's a place that strives to learn from its mistakes, and when it does, the rest of the world turns to it as a role model. This is why Singapore's passport is the strongest, its seaport is the second busiest, its water is the cleanest, its airport is the greatest, its landfills are the prettiest, and its people are the friendliest.

And here's a place where no less than the prime minister of the country, Lee Hsien Loong, broke into a big smile when he heard that Nas Daily was paying a visit to his beloved land, and he agreed to appear on camera just to tell us that the work never stops. "This is what we have been building in Singapore for fifty-three years," he said proudly, "and we will be building it for many more years to come."

THE PLASTIC STRAW DILEMMA

Yesterday, I bought a drink at McDonald's, but it was served to me without a straw.

"Excuse me," I said to the cashier, "does this come with a straw?"

"Sorry, but we don't use plastic straws," she responded.

"Why not?" I asked.

"Because McDonald's wants to protect the environment," she said proudly, "so we've banned the use of plastic straws."

I was impressed. I like green-minded people, and I especially appreciated hearing this bit of activism coming from a representative of a huge corporation like McDonald's.

But then I looked down at my cup and saw that it still had a plastic lid. And I looked over at the tables and saw a guy eating his salad with a plastic fork. And I looked at the woman next to him, stirring her coffee with a plastic stirrer. And then I saw a bunch of guys chowing down on their Quarter Pounders—which are made of meat, which comes from animal agriculture, which is responsible for 15 percent of the world's greenhouse gas emissions.

Fifteen percent.

All of which begs the question: Why does McDonald's care so much about sparing the planet its beach-littering, turtle-choking, nonbiodegradable plastic straws but it ignores the countless other ways the corporation is harming the planet?

The answer is something called "selective empathy."

This is a problem all humans suffer from. We selectively care about one thing, yet we don't care about the other. Put another way, it would be like carefully sorting your kitchen trash for recycling, and as you're taking it out to the curb, you nonchalantly flick your cigarette onto your neighbor's lawn. Where's the consistency?

It's terrific that McDonald's wants to save that turtle from getting a straw stuck in its throat, but the same company doesn't blink an eye about selling a billion pounds of beef a year. That's five and a half million dead cattle. That's selective empathy in action.

And worst of all, we're not aware of our own fickle activism. The same people who express horror at, say, the Chinese eating dogmeat are often the same people who go home and fire up a nice, juicy lamb chop. We feel empathy for the pooch but not for the lamb. That means, around the world, we have slaughterhouse workers bumping off millions of sheep every day, then cuddling with their puppies when they get home.

"Well, at least we're not doing that with *people*," we rationalize. "We would never be so selectively empathic with humans, right?" Wrong. It is said that all people are created equal, but do we care about all people equally? I was personally devastated by the murder of Saudi journalist Jamal Khashoggi in 2018, but was I just as concerned about the thirty thousand innocents killed in war-torn Yemen that same year? No, I wasn't. Why is that? Because I'm guilty of selective empathy, too.

This is nothing new. More than half a century ago, Soviet hard-liner Joseph Stalin, one of history's more despised villains, was responsible for the deaths of as many as twenty million people. "A single death is a tragedy, a million deaths is a statistic," he reportedly said at the time. Whether or not those shocking words actually came out of the dictator's mouth, the sentiment pretty much hits the ugly nail on its ugly head. That's the way a lot of people think.

As I sat there sipping my McDonald's drink with no straw, surrounded by meat and more plastic, I couldn't help but ask myself, "Do we really care about plastic? About animals? About humans? Or do we only care about *some* plastic, *some* animals, and *some* humans?" These are questions worth asking, no matter how uncomfortable they are to answer.

Keeping one plastic straw out of the environment is good, but caring about the larger problem is better.

FREE AT LAST

ZIMBABWE, DAY 600

On November 29, 2017, I was in a great mood. Nas Daily had just reached Day 600, and my videos had surpassed 450 million views. The very fantasy I'd conjured a year and a half earlier—grinding out one video every day and never missing a post—was still in full throttle, and I was ready to celebrate.

And celebrate I did, joining a party that was already in progress—and sixteen million strong. That's because the party had nothing to do with me, or Nas Daily, or anything remotely connected to the world of social media. The celebration was for the nation of Zimbabwe, which only days earlier had

thrown off an oppressive dictator who had ruled the country with an iron fist for more than thirty-seven years.

Landlocked on the southern peninsula of Africa, between the graceful curves of the Zambezi and Limpopo rivers, Zimbabwe is renowned for its magnificent wildlife and cinematic landscapes. It also possesses a history that, in many ways, embodies both the triumphs and tragedies of other African nations. For a thousand years it was the province of various kingdoms and governmental states, and envied by European and Arab merchants and traders for its rich natural resources—gold, ivory, and copper. It was explored and plundered, occupied and colonized, like so many of its neighbors on the continent.

But in 1965, its minority-white government declared the country independent, renaming it Rhodesia and sending it into fifteen years of global isolation and guerrilla rebellion. That instability is what allowed Robert Mugabe to seize power in 1980; and for the next thirty-seven years, he locked the country into an endless spiral of economic decline, class warfare, and human rights violations. All of that came to an end on November 15, 2017—twelve days before my plane touched down on Zimbabwean soil—when nationwide demonstrations and a coup d'état by the country's army finally brought an end to Mugabe's dictatorial reign, sending the people of this beautiful African nation into an exuberant frenzy.

NOVEMBER 2017: JUBILATION IN ZIMBABWE

When I arrived in Harare, the capital city, Zimbabweans were still danc-ing in the streets.

"Welcome to Zimbabwe!" I told my viewers, as locals swarmed around me, proudly waving the nation's flag. "You probably know this country for its old dictator, Robert Mugabe, who just a few days ago was overthrown—and all of this was done with zero bullets, zero casualties, and a lot of peaceful protestors!"

As the old song goes, I don't know much about history, but I've become somewhat fluent in the language of hope. And what I saw upon my arrival in Zimbabwe was a defiantly optimistic people. They did not look angry, they did not look worried—they looked proud.

I trained my camera on the many jubilant Zimbabweans who streamed by me on the street and asked them how they felt.

"I am so happy today!" said one.

"I feel free now!" said another.

"It is a new era and a new beginning!" said a third.

This is what is called "the power of the people," and when I posted the video that night on Facebook, I titled it "The Happiest Nation in the World." And that's really how it felt.

But thirty-seven years is a long time, and I was deeply curious about how Zimbabwe would find its way back to stability from nearly four decades of dictatorial rule. Over the next few days I probed that question, and it didn't take me very long to learn Zimbabwe's secret to survival: ingenuity.

Take, for example, their ride-sharing system. We all know of Uber and Lyft and Via, and all those ride-hailing apps created by well-paid software engineers in their cushy offices in San Francisco. Turns out, the same "tech-nology" existed in Zimbabwe. Faced with a collapsed economy and skyrock-eting employment, some Zimbabweans figured out a way to create their own ride-sharing community—and workforce—that doesn't rely on technology. It's called Mushika-shika (which in Zimbabwe's native language of Shona is slang for "Quick, quick!"), and it operates just like Uber, only without the app. It's a network of people with their own cars who patrol the streets like a feisty fleet of shuttles and will take you to your destination for much cheaper fares than taxis—they'll even pick up more passengers along the way, just like an Uber pool. The cost? Fifty cents a ride. In fact, the San Francisco–based company Lyft used to be called Zimride, because the founder had been in

Zimbabwe and witnessed the very Mushika-shika that I watched in action. He went on to make Lyft a multibillion-dollar company.

Granted, Mushika-shika is a little more seat-of-the-pants than Uber, and some locals—including the media and the police—consider it a dangerous menace. I find that so interesting. If you look a bit closer at the criticism, you'll see that it comes largely from the elite—the top percentage of society. But from what I witnessed, the people of Zimbabwe love Mushika-shika and use it left and right.

Yet even if the whole operation was shut down tomorrow, I can't help but see a certain hopefulness in grassroots efforts like Mushika-shika. Here are ordinary citizens rebounding from decades of government oppression and creating their own jobs, all while helping to make each other's lives better. Sometimes, I reminded myself, innovation comes from where you least expect it.

Zimbabweans are similarly inventive when it comes to their money-exchange system. While I was in Harare, I ran out of cash; and because the government screwed up the economy so badly, the banks were a nightmare and none of the ATMs worked. But the people of Zimbabwe have found a way around this chaos by putting their wallets inside their phones. The system is called EcoCash, and it's a countrywide method of paying or receiving money electronically. Launched in 2011—right there in Zimbabwe—EcoCash allows its users to deposit, withdraw, transfer, or spend funds through their mobile devices. That means that whatever dough you have exists as a balance on

MUSHIKA-SHIKA

ECOCASH

your phone, which increases and decreases according to your spending and saving—so cash is no longer king.

This topic is near and dear to me because my first job out of college was at Venmo, which by then had become a dominant player in the American mobile payments industry. It was a brilliant app, but man, getting street vendors to accept it was close to impossible. In Zimbabwe, however, EcoCash is accepted everywhere. You can use it in restaurants and for lodging, street parking, and highway fruit vendors—you can even give a handout to someone who's homeless with just a tap of a button.

Will Mushika-shika and EcoCash rescue this underdeveloped country with a collapsed economy and a dysfunctional government? Of course not. But I still find it inspiring that in a world dominated by a handful of superpowers, we can learn lessons from countries that are not doing so well but trying hard to do better.

I flew out of Zimbabwe on Day 603, headed for Swaziland, Johannesburg, and points beyond. When I'd arrived at the airport in Harare, it was just after dinnertime; the skies were deep indigo, and I couldn't help but notice how desolate the place was. It was also very quiet.

"Guys," I said to my camera in a whisper, "I have just arrived at what has to be the loneliest, creepiest airport in the world. I'm the only one in the customs line, the only one at the passport check, the only one at security, and the only one entering the terminal. My flight, meanwhile, is just one of six flying out of Zimbabwe today, and only thirty other people are booked on the plane. What's happening here?"

I wasn't kidding—I actually found the place spooky. This was an international airport in the capital of an entire nation, and yet I was surrounded by this surreal stillness. I'd just spent three days in Zimbabwe, talking about its newfound freedom and the robust spirit of its people. But it wasn't until I looked at the footage of that barren airport that I began to comprehend the problems confronting the country.

The experience made me think. Maybe the next time we all get stuck in a busy airport, instead of growing frustrated by the long lines and the nosy TSA people and the shoulder-to-shoulder crowds at the gates, we should pause for a moment and be grateful that what we're witnessing are the fruits of a healthy economy and a functioning government—things that Zimbabwe does not yet enjoy.

I wish the country a *mushika-shika* road to recovery.

FROM FAKE NEWS TO FENG SHUI

CHINA, DAY 891

This is not going to be a friendly chapter.

China scares me. In fact, it was one of the few countries—perhaps the *only* country—I visited over the course of a thousand days that frightened me so much I considered not going there. I'm not typically an avoidance kind of guy,

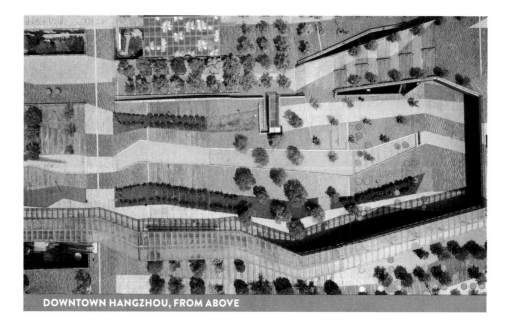

DOWNTOWN HANGZHOU, FROM ABOVE

but China has crossed the line a few too many times in recent years, making it sort of impossible not to be wary of it.

I'll explain.

If you pay attention to the news even occasionally, you already know why a lot of people resent China. It's secretive. It's isolated. It's sullen. And it's a huge player on the international stage that hasn't quite learned to play by the rules.

For starters, the country has shown little regard for intellectual property. During my relatively short time there, I saw entire technology stores filled with fake products. Shelf after shelf of copycat knockoffs sold at bargain prices, and nobody seemed to think there was anything wrong with that. Phones, laptops, desktops—all of them direct lifts from Apple, only without the little apple logo on the case.

And it wasn't only electronics. I saw cars that were exact copies of Teslas, sneakers that were complete rip-offs of Air Jordans, even an entire city that was a replica of Paris. Yes, you read that right. China copies so much that it copied Paris. *Mon dieu!*

The internet in China is also problematic. It's a lot less free and a lot more censored than the web we're used to in the West. Facebook? WhatsApp? Google? They're all blocked in China, which made my time there significantly harder. The government is also notoriously good at substituting real headlines with propaganda. How do you say "fake news" in Chinese?

Then there's the discrimination. The country's treatment of Muslims in western China is deeply disturbing, to say the least. We've all read the stories about China's lack of respect for human rights in general, but its disdain for Muslims is particularly cruel. According to the *New York Times*, in the city of Hotan alone, hundreds of Uighur Muslims are penned in behind barbed wire, where they undergo a "high-pressure indoctrination program" to condition them to adore Communism. I chose not to visit Hotan, for obvious reasons.

And last but not least: dogs. While I didn't witness it personally, it is still believed that people eat dogs in China—an allegation that continues to piss off myriad animal lovers in the West. I asked a few locals about this, and I was told it was "mostly" rumor—that only a small portion of the population actually eats dogs. If that's the case, it's still one more thing that leaves the average visitor troubled by the country.

So clearly, I wasn't a big fan of China when I boarded my flight to Beijing. But once I arrived there, I made the commitment to create videos the same way I'd done in all of the other countries I visited. I reported candidly and honestly about what I saw. And to my relief, I walked away with a fair measure of respect for the Chinese people.

At 3.6 million square miles, with a population of 1.4 billion, China has a lot to look at. From its glimmering harbors to its rural villages, it is achingly picturesque. And its rich history—one that spans more than four thousand years of kingdoms and dynasties and wars—is equally compelling. But perhaps the one thing that will remain forever seared in my brain about China is the way it builds.

On Day 892, I visited Hangzhou, the busy capital city of Zhejiang Province that lies on the serene bay between Shanghai and Ningbo. Famous for its tea and silk, Hangzhou made its mark in days of old as a favorite trading post, especially among Arab merchants (shout-out to my peeps!). But today the city is recognized as the pulsing heart of Zhejiang's economy, politics, and culture, and it is one of the fastest-growing cities in the world. That's what pulled me there.

When I arrived in Hangzhou, it was night, and I was stopped in my tracks by three brightly lit buildings. The InterContinental hotel is a luxury five-star property that sits on the water's edge. Standing more than twenty stories, it was designed to resemble the sun—a perfect globe, plated in bright, sparkling gold. Imagine what Darth Vader's Death Star would look like if it weren't dark and evil. That's the InterContinental.

Just across the street from the hotel is the Hangzhou Grand Theater, which is no less a masterpiece. Set on a one-million-square-foot plaza, it's home to an opera house, a concert hall, and an open-air stage. But it is the theater's exterior that's the real eye-grabber: a curved, pool-blue glass skin that was sculpted in the shape of a crescent moon.

And just two thousand feet away, across the lazy Qiantang River, is the Hangzhou Citizen's Center, a towering complex of six gracefully curved high-rises arranged in a circle and connected by sky bridges three hundred feet in the air. If you think the towers resemble six humans standing in an intimate

HANGZHOU AT NIGHT

huddle, their arms gently draped around one another, you're right. It was built to look that way.

So there you have it. The Sun. The Moon. Humanity. What's the big deal?

The big deal is that the buildings are communicating with each other.

See, in China, people believe in the power of energy. Good energy brings success, and bad energy brings failure. And these three buildings in Hangzhou were constructed—and positioned—in a way that turbocharges the good and sends the bad packing. The architects and planners placed the sun building and the moon building across from one another to attract the river's good energy, which in turn flows through them and then whips back out to the six tall guys in the group hug. Once it circles them, the energy is then beamed out across the entire city, sending its good vibes along with it.

In another words, China spent a billion dollars to invite an invisible force from the water to flow through its proud skyscrapers before embarking on a citywide journey. Talk about energy efficiency.

This is not fake news. This is feng shui, the ancient Chinese science of geomancy, which claims that the positioning of objects—from forests to buildings—can harness energy in a way that helps people harmonize with their environment.

And in Hangzhou, feng shui is apparently working. That's why the city kicks ass. Its shopping malls are built to generate the same energy flow to attract more business. Twin towers are erected with open spaces between them so that energy swims through those gaps. The more good energy in the air, the better our lives are.

And feng shui isn't just in China—it's all over the world. You can see it in the Singapore skyline. You can see it on the Hong Kong landscape. You can even see it in your home. Yep, many people arrange their furniture according to the principles of feng shui. Your bed, your sofa, your mirror, your TV—all of them can be arranged in a way that soaks your place in good energy. That way, when you come home cranky and tired from a long day at work, you'll instantly be infused with peaceful positivity. You'd think it was magic if it weren't so real.

I left China on Day 897, headed for Hong Kong and then Canada. I still harbored the same reservations I'd had on my arrival, but they were softened by a sense of respect for the Chinese, who are looking to the future. The most important thing I'd learned during my stay was that good energy, in any form, matters. We all need more good energy in our lives—from our friends, from our living rooms, from our buildings, and from our governments. China has some of that figured out.

FENG SHUI IN HANGZHOU (CLOCKWISE FROM TOP): THE INTERCONTINENTAL, THE GRAND THEATER, THE CITIZEN'S CENTER

When someone is arrested at the age of fourteen, it's hard to imagine him having a happy life. Now imagine he was arrested *seven more times*. Yet the story of Bashar Masri is different. Raised in Nablus, Palestine, on the country's volatile West Bank, Bashar felt it his duty to protest the occupation of his homeland by the Israeli government in 1967. "I used to throw rocks," he told me, "but they didn't go very far." They went far enough, however, for the Israeli Army to toss Bashar in jail eight times. But his story doesn't end there. Bashar went on to the United States, where he graduated from Virginia Tech with a degree in engineering. But he never forgot the struggles back home, which is why he returned to Palestine, where he created or invested in thirty different businesses—from real estate to agriculture—amassing billions along the way. That's when Bashar threw his support behind the two-state solution for Palestine and Israel by building Rawabi, an awesome high-tech city rising from the hills of the West Bank. The largest real estate project in Palestinian history, Rawabi boasts six thousand units capable of housing forty thousand individuals and providing jobs for ten thousand of his people. All these years after his first arrest, Bashar is no longer throwing rocks, but using them to build a future for his beloved homeland.

CYPRUS A MIRACULOUS FRIENDSHIP

Forty-four years ago, Cyprus was engulfed in conflict, and soldiers from the north and south were called to action in the town of Lefka. Among those fighters were Yiannis Maratheftis, a Greek Cypriot, and Fathi Akinci, a Turkish Cypriot. Yiannis (right, below) was just nineteen years old and hoping the battle would be brief; it was his last day serving in the Greek Army. But his luck was short-lived: he was shot in the head by Fathi, who watched the young soldier's helmet and radio tumble to the ground, convincing him he was dead. Miraculously, though, Yiannis survived the injury, married, and built a family.

Thirty-four years later, Yiannis's story was featured in a book about the war in Cyprus. A Turkish translation found its way to Fathi, who was shocked to learn that the man he'd left for dead was still alive. Fathi reached out to Yiannis and asked for forgiveness, and the two men decided to meet. It was an emotional moment. The last time they'd been together, they were pointing guns at each other. This time, they embraced. Today, Yiannis and Fathi remain close friends who regularly cross the country's military border to spend time with each other's families—bringing gifts of fruit and smiles. They still remain soldiers in their hearts, but now instead of fighting each other, they are fighting together for peace.

CHINA THE FAKE PARIS

It might have been the most romantic date ever. Alyne wore a long red gown, I was in my formal Nas Daily T-shirt, and there we were, frolicking in the City of Love—Paris! We danced up the Champs-Élysées, posed for selfies in front of the Eiffel Tower, then ducked into a dreamy little café and ordered . . . *moo shu vegetables*? That's right, we weren't anywhere near the French capital, but rather in Tianducheng, the fake Paris of China. In 2007, developers began construction on this *incroyable* imposter, which is located in the suburbs of Hangzhou, just a sixty-minute bullet train ride from Shanghai. The effort was part of a nationwide real estate boom that was bracing for China's population explosion—and, *sacré bleu*, it's a beaut! In addition to the impressive 1:3 scale replica of the Eiffel Tower, everything else is a pitch-perfect copycat—from the charming apartment houses to the quaint storefronts to the counterfeit fountain at the phony Luxembourg Gardens. But there was one little problem: nobody showed up. Now China's answer to Paris is a virtual ghost town—the apartments are vacant, the shops are shuttered, and the pretty, tree-lined boulevards are noticeably *sans touristes*. As that old movie line goes, "We'll always have Paris"—and the brain trust behind Tianducheng pulled that off to perfection. Let's just hope that in the coming years, China's valentine to Europe's most amorous city gets the visitors it deserves. Otherwise, as they say along the Seine, *c'est la vie*.

INDIA **THE HOLIEST WATERS ON EARTH**

On my second trip to India, I traveled to Varanasi, the holiest city in all of Hinduism, located in the northern state of Uttar Pradesh. As a visitor in a foreign land, I was captivated by its mystical spirit; as a Muslim, I could barely wrap my head around it. Varanasi sits on the banks of the legendary river Ganges, whose dark-green waters are sacred to the country's Hindus. Millions have traveled to the Ganges to wash their sins away, believing that the spiritual power of the river will make them pure. And if you die near the Ganges, locals told me, you will attain *moksha*, an eternal state of enlightenment and a liberation from the cycle of death and rebirth. During my two days in Varanasi, I watched hundreds of devout Hindus pray to the river god in elaborate rituals, and I waded into the waters of the Ganges myself. I witnessed the nightly cremation of dead bodies, the flames from the charnel grounds painting the black sky with spikes of yellow. I lingered beside Hindu ascetics, who rub the ashes of the dead on their bodies, eat flesh from human corpses, and fashion the bones into jewelry and skullcaps. At one point as I sat by this holy river, I was rendered speechless as a dead body floated by me. In an instant, my entire life, my journey, felt so small and insignificant compared to the mammoth scale of the diverse religions, beliefs, and traditions of our world. Varanasi was one of the most raw, human, chaotic places I've ever visited, and yet I found it to be one of the most peaceful, too.

ISRAEL **THE LANGUAGE OF PEACE**

In 2012, Liron Lavi Turkenich made a startling discovery about her own reading habits: whenever she looked at the street signage in her hometown of Haifa, Israel—which, as in much of the country, includes both Hebrew and Arabic words—she ignored the Arabic. That didn't sit well with her. "In Haifa," she told me, "these two cultures exist as parallel lines; they are side by side, but never touch. I wanted to make these lines meet, so I decided to design a new typeface. Letters are my tools." To create her font, Liron, thirty-four, drew on the research of nineteenth-century French ophthalmologist Louis Émile Javal, who discovered that the human eye need only see the top half of Latin letters to identify the words they spell. This also applied to Arabic letters, and through trial and error, Liron discovered that the same held true for the bottom half of Hebrew letters. So in a painstaking process that took up to fifteen hours per word, Liron split the letters in half and sewed the right parts together, creating a 638-character alphabet that could be instantly recognized by speakers of both Arabic and Hebrew. She called it Aravrit, and it has literally rewritten the

way the people of Haifa coexist. "I never intended for Aravrit to become political," Liron told me, "but it sends a message to all of us—Jews and Arab Israelis, Israelis and Palestinians—that by not ignoring the other, we are acknowledging our coexistence. This is what creates real change—in our own minds and, hopefully, in society."

PART 8
OUR AMAZING PLANET

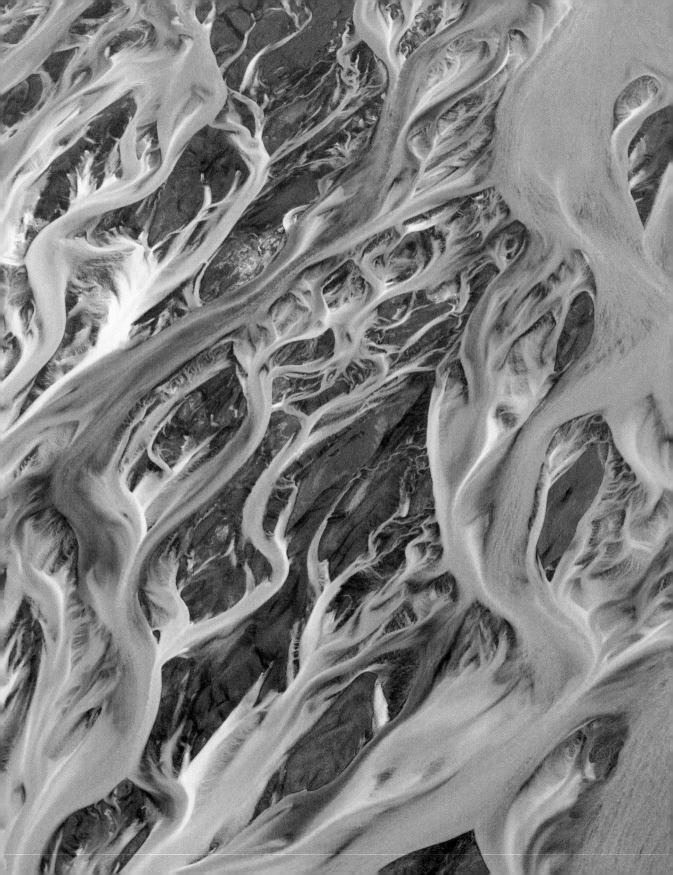

THERE'S A NINTH PLANET

ICELAND, DAY 792

When I was a kid, I was taught that there are eight planets in the solar system. So imagine my surprise when, all these years later, I discovered that there is a ninth planet after all. And here's the kicker: it's hiding right here on Earth.

It's called Planet Iceland.

It was Day 792, and I'd just left the comparatively warm climes of Denmark, heading due northwest over the North Atlantic. My destination was the volcanically active, geyser-riddled, glacier-rich island country of Iceland—a Nordic wonderland best known for its geographical isolation and cold-as-hell climate.

It took me only a day on Planet Iceland to begin cataloging the many things that made it different from any place I'd ever been. For one thing, it has no military (who needs a military when you're never at war with anyone?). It also has gender equality, top-notch air quality, excellent health care, high wages, and a low crime rate. What it doesn't have is mosquitoes. Or McDonald's. Or hate, for the most part.

Oh, and by the way, Iceland has an indigenous language that's as cool as the climate. When spoken, Icelandic sounds almost like music. *Það er eina mínútu, sjáumst á morgun!* means "That's one minute, see you tomorrow!"

But best of all, Iceland is rarely in the news—meaning it's the ideal destination for anyone trying to escape the round-the-clock drumbeat of global doom

ICELAND'S LANDSCAPES: FROM GLACIERS TO VALLEYS TO BLACK BEACHES

GEOTHERMAL POWER PLANT IN ICELAND

and gloom. This is not to suggest that the country is some backward-looking Podunk, mindlessly shoveling snow up there on the hem of the Arctic Circle. To the contrary, this sparkling forty-thousand-square-mile slab of mountain, valley, and glacier just likes to mind its own business as it goes about the very important task of being a smart, healthy, and progressive country.

Case in point: You go into your bathroom in the morning and run the shower, and the first thing you notice is the smell of rotten eggs. Okay, not the most inviting way to greet the day, but it's your first sign that you're on a friendly planet that's looking out for you. That's because that hot water in your shower (and in showers in many parts of Iceland) comes directly from the island's bubbling hot springs—the ones that fuel those dazzling geysers— and is delivered right to your home by geothermal power plants. That not only saves you from having to buy an expensive boiler, but the sulfur in the water—the source of that bad-egg smell—is also believed to fight a variety of ailments, from arthritis to skin disease.

Your cold water, meanwhile, comes from a completely different source— the island's natural springs—and many consider it to be the freshest and cleanest water on earth. In fact, at the popular diving site at Iceland's Silfra fissure, the only place on the planet where you can dive between two tectonic plates, you can actually drink the water you're snorkeling in.

And I'm not done yet. Icelandic water is also helping to save the environment. Instead of spewing fossil fuels and other pollutants into the atmosphere like most of its global neighbors, Iceland produces all of its electricity through hydropower, harnessing its rivers and hot springs and glaciers to grow vegetables in greenhouses, water them, and, while they're at it, light up the entire country.

Those glaciers, by the way, are a trip. True to its name, 11 percent of the country is made up of glacial ice—the largest of the glaciers being Vatnajökull, which covers three thousand square miles and, in some places, is half a mile thick. That's one seriously big hunk of ice. I wasn't in the country more than a few days before Alyne and I took a hike on one of those babies, and the experience was transcendent. Half of my brain was focused on trying to keep my spiked boots firmly planted in the ice beneath me, while the other half was flipping out that I was actually walking on top of water that was hundreds of thousands of years old. Clearly, I wasn't in Arraba anymore, Toto.

Over the course of my twelve days in Iceland, I collected ample evidence that the country is a planet of its own. The sun there, for example, is very particular about when it shows its face. In the summer, it never gets dark, and in the winter, it's nighttime all the time. Given that I visited in June, the sky was constantly happy and bright, so my inner clock went crazy. I don't sleep a lot—typically five or six hours a night—but I tend to need a moon for my shut-eye, and one was never in view there.

THE ICELANDIC HORSE, STRAIGHT OUT OF PIXAR

ICELAND'S VIKINGS: A SPECIES OF THEIR OWN

And the list of oddities goes on: The beaches in Iceland are black. The horses are short and squat—like adorable Pixar characters—and trot with an equally cartoony gait. And then there's Iceland's famous penis museum, where hundreds of mammal johnsons are on perpetual exhibit.

As for the people of Iceland, they're definitely a species of their own. They descended from the Vikings, which means they possess a robust steeliness that gives them the strength and confidence to live in such an extreme environment—to develop it, to build homes in it, and to embrace a culture that, like the water there, has been untouched for centuries.

And everyone has their own story to tell. I met a beautiful young couple who were very much in love and hoped to marry—that is, until they discovered that they were related. I guess that's bound to happen when you all come from the same line of descendants.

I met Jón Gnarr, a national comedian who'd gotten so fed up with governmental politics that he decided to run for mayor of Reykjavík, Iceland's capital, as a joke. His campaign was a hoot, as he hit the stump promising the nation free towels, a polar bear, and its own Disneyland. The punch line? He won.

And, of course, I met hundreds of Icelanders who flocked to my meetups with gusto and a palpable pride in their country. You don't paint the national flag on your face and don those Viking horns unless you really mean it.

Maybe it was the mood I was in, maybe it was all that fresh air blowing the clutter from my head, but on my tenth day in Iceland I decided to put together a special four-minute segment that featured a medley of all the amazing things I witnessed on that frozen plot of earth, and my feelings about them.

"This is by far the hardest, most expensive video I've made," I told my viewers when I posted it, "and I couldn't be any prouder to share it with you. But it isn't a travel video," I warned. "It's a peek into another world that does things differently—a land that makes you wish that all of Planet Earth could be as developed, as energy efficient, and as peaceful as this strange and beautiful planet."

The responses to the video were instant and gratifying.

"I'm so glad you're enjoying our country so much," wrote a local named Bryndis, punctuating her comment with a bright-yellow happy face. "We're so happy to have you here."

"Everyone knows McDonald's causes conflict," added Mike from Jerusalem. "That's Iceland's secret—no McDonald's, no war!"

But it was Deepanshu from India who best summed up viewer reactions to our spin around this remarkable ninth planet: "Bro, take me with you."

THE WONDER DOWN UNDER

Well, it took me long enough to get there.

On April 20, 2018—Day 742 of Nas Daily—my flight touched down in Australia, the only destination in my thousand days of travels that qualifies as a country, a commonwealth, and a continent all in one. I was thrilled to arrive, but getting there was a pain. More than a full year earlier I had applied

BROOME, AUSTRALIA, ON THE COUNTRY'S KIMBERLEY COAST

for a visa to enter the country, but I got rejected because the Australian government didn't consider making videos for Facebook a real job. Six months later I tried to pass through Australia en route to New Zealand—just a stopover, not an entry—and I got denied again. Obviously not taking the hint, I made a third attempt a few months later, and once more, I was treated to the Aussie equivalent of "Piss off, mate."

By this point I started to get the feeling that perhaps an entire nation just didn't like me and that maybe I'd have better luck trying to slink into a friendlier country—like North Korea. But in the spring of 2018, I decided to give it one more shot, and apparently four times was the charm. "Come on down!" they shouted.

Floating at the bottom of the world—twenty hours of flying time from most sane places on the planet—Australia is the poster child for geographic isolation, a three-million-square-mile symphony of shiny cities, parched deserts, lush rain forests, jagged mountain ranges, and lots of hard, flat soil, all surrounded by endless miles of ocean. It is also, in a way, a living snapshot of humankind, as its first inhabitants—the Aboriginal Australians, who still live there—paddled over from South Asia more than sixty thousand years ago, making the country one of the oldest human settlements on earth. Colonized by the British in the eighteenth century (still a sensitive topic among modern-day Australians), it claimed nationhood in 1901 and remains today a dominion of Great Britain. But from my observations, Australia is only as British as the small Union Jack that sits in the corner of its flag. Otherwise, it proudly lives up to its Outback cred, marching to the sound of its own Aussie drumbeat and inviting every visitor to fall in step. Which I did.

I began my journey through Australia probably the way everyone else does: getting used to the idea that the country is basically upside down. Water swirls down drains in the opposite direction of water in the Northern Hemisphere, cars drive on the "wrong" side of the road, and the weather is completely flipped—December is hot and July is cold.

But directionally speaking, Australia is actually one of the most forward-looking countries I visited. Contrary to the backwoods stereotype, Australia is a land of fierce thinkers who have made significant contributions to the modern age—from Wi-Fi to Google Maps to a vaccine to prevent cervical cancer—and its government welfare system is the envy of the globe.

And yet it was the Aussies themselves who impressed me the most.

RYAN HARTSHORN: HE MAKES VODKA FROM SHEEP

Case in point: In Tasmania, I met Ryan Hartshorn, a thirty-four-year-old cheese maker who, having grown bored with his job, taught himself to make vodka from sheep's milk. He's now a successful distiller.

I also met Campbell Remess, a fourteen-year-old boy who decided that life was all about helping others, so he taught himself to use his mother's sewing machine and began making colorful teddy bears to send to people around the world who could use a little bit of plush TLC—especially cancer patients, who need something to hug during their treatments. When I first met Campbell, he'd just shipped his fourteen thousandth teddy. They now go on eBay for thousands of dollars, which Campbell donates to charities.

I continued my Aussie expedition in the city of Melbourne, a cultural haven best known for its botanical gardens and world-class cricket ground. It was here that I got a crash course in Aussie slang. For example, a sandwich is a *sanga*, definitely is *defo*, breakfast is *brekkie*, and Australia is *Straya*. Sounds easy enough—until you hear someone say, "I'm defo gonna grab a sausage sanga, Straya-style, for brekkie," It takes some getting used to.

But, alas, Melbourne is also where I got my first—and last—taste of Vegemite, Australia's answer to torture. Vegemite is sold twenty-two million times every year in Australia, and I have no idea why. Originally invented as a condiment to be spread on toast, crumpets, and biscuits, it is probably best described as shit-in-a-jar and has gone on to earn worldwide notoriety for its sheer yuckiness. I think the big problem with Vegemite is that its deep-brown

MYSTERIOUS TIDES OF BROOME

hue and gooey texture trick you into believing it will taste like Nutella. But once your tongue makes contact with those special ingredients—leftover brewer's yeast extract, malt extract from barley, vegetable and spice additives, and other crap—you'll be convinced that this is your payback for doing something wrong in a previous life.

Once I'd recovered from my Vegemitis, I was ready for the most important leg of my Australian journey: a trek to Broome, the picturesque pearling town that sits on the country's northwestern Kimberley Coast. It was here that I met Aboriginals, whose population has now dwindled to a mere 3.3 percent of the country's inhabitants.

As with most indigenous peoples, the Aboriginals took the brunt of their land's colonization. With every new British flag that rose over Australia in the eighteenth and nineteenth centuries, the more the indigenous population lost their precious land—and their rights. As their numbers continued to shrink, the colonizers were even authorized to shoot the "natives" if they got in the way of white progress.

But over two hundred years, through a steady slog of protests, legislative battles, and government acts, the Aboriginals fought their way back to their rightful claim of the land they'd first settled. Like the Māori of New Zealand—or the Native Americans in the United States, for that matter—their numbers are small and their political sway is tenuous, but their pride of heritage remains the most powerful thing I saw on the continent.

Broome is in the middle of nowhere—an outpost in genuine Outback country, where endless stretches of red sand roads cut through the brush clear to the edge of the horizon, and beyond. The city is like any small town, with a Domino's Pizza on the main drag and a hundred-year-old open-air cinema house that sits at the edge of the water.

But one look at Broome's natural beauty and you can understand why the Aboriginals fought so hard to hold on to it. Here, the ocean tides are among the highest in the world, rising up to thirty feet. When the tide is in, you're standing on an island; when the tide moves out, the land becomes a desert, revealing dinosaur tracks that are 130 million years old. And the movement of the water is hypnotic: at low tide, waterfalls suddenly appear in the middle of the ocean as the seawater drains from the coral reefs. It's a natural phenomenon that I've never witnessed anywhere else on earth.

THE ROAD TO BROOME

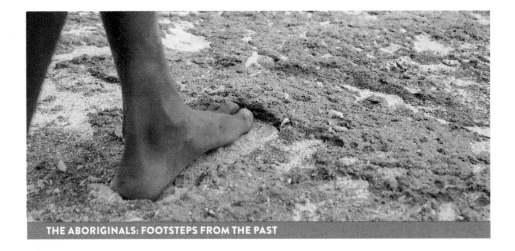

THE ABORIGINALS: FOOTSTEPS FROM THE PAST

These waters are where locals work the trade that Broome is known for—pearl agriculture—and during my one day there, I watched an enthusiastic band of pearl farmers gather enough pearls from oysters to make a necklace that could easily sell for $15,000 on Fifth Avenue. And every one of those pearls was perfect.

Just as stunning as Broome's magnificent seascapes are the skies above it, which are clear three hundred days of the year, producing the most romantic sunsets I've ever seen. And because this part of Australia has no light pollution, the night heavens explode with stars and galaxies as far as the eye can see.

But what I'll remember best are the Aboriginal people who live under those stars. Their ancestors first stepped onto the continent tens of thousands of years ago; and if you're lucky enough to get Aboriginals to tell you their family stories—which I was—they'll teach you a few words in their own language and show you the footprints of some of their ancient relatives, which are still imbedded in the rocks.

Just hold on to that for a second and think about it. Here is a tiny town in the Australian Outback that is not only graced by some of the world's most magnificent displays of nature—from waterfalls and pearls, to dinosaurs and sunsets—but is also still home to the oldest living human culture on the planet.

Yeah, I may have been given the runaround about coming to visit, but after three weeks in *Straya*, it was *defo* worth the hassle.

AM I A BAD MUSLIM?

Over the past few years, I've gotten a lot of criticism for being a bad Muslim. No matter what country I'm reporting from, or who I'm hanging out with, or what I'm doing at any given moment, there's always a handful of finger-waggers on my Facebook page, primed and ready to throw the Quran at me.

When I visited the gay capital of the world—the Castro in San Francisco—and celebrated the freedom that the LGBTQ community enjoys there, I was called a bad Muslim.

When I sampled a few beers in Prague on a one-day stopover from Romania to Ukraine (the cheapest brewskis I've ever bought, by the way!), I was called a bad Muslim.

When I reported on the prostitution trade in Senegal and marveled at the way it was supported by the government, I was called a bad Muslim.

And don't even get me started on the snide comments about my girlfriend.

If it isn't obvious by now, I'm not a religious Muslim, but I'm also not a bad one. I embrace some components of Islam and reject others—but even with its flaws, I find it a beautiful faith. And I never force my beliefs on others.

I don't oppose religious freedoms or ideas, and I expect the same respect in return.

And I never, ever criticize others for their faith.

Good Muslims—or good Christians or Jews or Hindus or atheists, for that matter—are people who have an intimate relationship with their beliefs, but keep it to themselves. We pray to God one-on-one, so why should anyone else intrude on that most personal of conversations?

If you want to change the world for the better—which many religions aspire to do—then lead by example, not by wrist-slapping those who disagree with you.

My personal credo—religious, secular, and otherwise—is "live and let live." That's always served me well. At the end of the day, I'm always reminded of what the Prophet Muhammad said: "The best among you is the one who doesn't harm others with his tongue and hands." That's something worth remembering.

MI LAIKIM KANTRI!

PAPUA NEW GUINEA, DAY 856

When I was a kid and saw a map of the world for the first time, I was wildly disappointed.

"The whole planet has already been explored!" I whined to my dad. "Look! Every country already has a name on it. There are even names on all those tiny islands in the middle of the ocean. There's nothing left to explore!"

It was an innocent observation for a little kid, but I was proved wrong on Day 856 of Nas Daily, when I arrived in Papua New Guinea, which is often referred to as one of the least explored places on the globe.

Occupying the eastern half of the massive island of New Guinea (the second largest island in the world, after Greenland), Papua New Guinea floats serenely in the Southern Hemisphere—Australia to its south, Indonesia to its west, and about thirty-three million square miles of Pacific Ocean to its east. Its eight million citizens are spread among more than a thousand social groups that are descended from hundreds of tribes, clans, and ethnicities, making it one of the most heterogeneous populations on the planet. It is also a topographical wonderland, graced with rugged mountains, thick rain forests, temperamental volcanoes, and sixteen hundred miles of stunning coastal beaches.

And yet its very remoteness—geographically and culturally—makes Papua New Guinea almost impossible to fully explore. In fact, some scientists even suspect that undiscovered species of animals and plants still live within its borders.

But it's the people of Papua New Guinea who are the toughest to categorize. Most of them live in tribes on mountaintops—far away from everyone else—so there is no uniform way of life, and some tribal customs take longer than others to die off. It wasn't until 1933 that seashells were abolished nationally as a form of currency.

And then there's the matter of language, which I could barely wrap my head around. More than eight hundred languages are spoken in the country, making it the most linguistically diverse place on earth; and each of those native tongues traces back to indigenous tribes and communities that have existed on Papua New Guinea for millennia.

That blew me away. I grew up knowing three languages—Arabic, Hebrew, and English—and I used to think that was impressive. But on Papua New Guinea, I'd be considered average, as most of the locals I met spoke from three to five languages.

And yet it is because of that crazy cacophony of tongues that the people of Papua New Guinea have adopted a simplified language, so that everybody can understand everybody else. It's called Tok Pisin—or Pidgin English to Westerners—and it's a colorful creole stew concocted from bits of Malay, Portuguese, German, English, and good old-fashioned shorthand. It was introduced to the locals by eighteenth-century colonizers and missionaries, which is never pretty to contemplate, given that languages should come from within a culture, rather than be imposed from outside. But over the centuries, the Papua New Guineans have made Tok Pisin their own, and today it is the most widely spoken language in the country.

The rules for Tok Pisin are pretty simple: its alphabet has twenty-two letters instead of twenty-six, and there are no long words, no arcane spellings, no hard grammar, and no insanely constructed sentences. In other words, it's every schoolkid's dream language.

Instead of "coffee" you say *kofi*.

Instead of "library," you say *buk haus* (book house).

"University" is *bik skul* (big school), "jungle" is *bik bus* (big bush), "eat" is *kaikaim*, and "dinner" is *nait kaikaim* (night eat).

Meanwhile, there aren't any of those stupid verb conjugations that make you want to bang a dictionary over your head. Instead of "I am," "she is," and "we are," it's simply *mi*, *yu*, and *ol* (me, you, and all).

Even the signage in Papua New Guinea is simpler than in other parts of the world, thanks to Tok Pisin. "Please Do Not Enter This Area" is shortened to *Yu No Ken Kam Insait*, while "No Smoking Is Permitted on These Premises" is the much less wordy *No Ken Simuk!*

The only Tok Pisin translation that didn't really seem all that different to me was *Yu luk nais* for "You look nice."

When I posted my video about Tok Pisin on Facebook, I framed it in a fun and lighthearted way, but secretly, I was moved in ways I didn't mention. By then I had already made a couple of laps around the planet, and in those travels I had begun to realize that the majority of our world's woes are rooted in miscommunication. Whether it's war among African nations or the raging infighting in the Middle East or the impoverished populations around the globe calling for help, it always comes down to our inability to really hear one another. So any country that tries to figure out a language that all of us can understand is a pretty great place in my book.

That's why I spent the majority of my time in Papua New Guinea in full investigation mode. During my week there, I dove deep into whatever customs and rituals I came across, and the people of this remarkable land were always eager to educate me.

I participated in "sing-sings," in which villagers paint themselves in dazzling colors and dress in elaborate costumes of shells, feathers, and animal skins to portray birds and mountain spirits.

I hung out with the "Mudmen" of the Asaro tribe in the eastern highlands, who coat their bodies in gray mud and wear scary devil masks made from melted pebbles in a lively reenactment of the legend of their tribal ancestors, who two hundred years ago drove enemies from their village by disguising themselves as angry, vengeful spirits.

I sampled the betel nut, a fruit from palm trees that is a favorite delicacy in South Asia and the tropical Pacific but in Papua New Guinea is spiced with tasty dashes of mustard seed and lime. Betel is addictive and potentially dangerous (the World Health Organization classifies it as a carcinogen), but it's an obsession with Papua New Guineans and always leaves the telltale "red mouth" on whoever samples it.

I cuddled with a pig, which, given that I'm a Muslim who doesn't eat pork—let alone touch the animal it comes from—was about as far outside my comfort zone as you can get. But in Papua New Guinea, pigs are sacred luxury items that are used to pay for brides, settle disputes, buy as an investment, or,

WEDDING DAY IN PAPUA NEW GUINEA

alas, consume on holidays. Your average porker in the country can run you as high as $1,300—or the cost of an iPhone—and because they play such an important role in the lives of the local people, I knew I had to get up-close and personal with one of them. I'm glad I did, but I probably won't be repeating the experience any time soon.

And to truly experience the local culture, my new friends helped me arrange a local wedding. I married Alyne in a full-blown Papua New Guinean ceremony. For the record, it was only a mock wedding (similar to our faux nuptials in India a year earlier), but that didn't keep us from pulling out all the stops. We both had our faces painted in vibrant tribal colors—the yellow paint extracted from a boiled rock, the black from ashes, the white from riverbed clay. We wore traditional wedding outfits made entirely from nature—grass-and-shell ensembles topped with wild headdresses (Alyne's headgear was a towering explosion of feathers; mine looked more like a small parade float). And in keeping with custom, instead of exchanging rings, I gave her a pig.

To be honest, Alyne and I felt a little like imposters in our wedding attire, but we must have pulled it off because everyone kept telling us, "*Yu luk nais.*"

And that, I think, was the true reward of the experience. These joyful villagers, living on one of the most remote outposts on the planet, took us in as members of their own tribe, no questions asked. They danced and sang throughout the day, demonstrating that they genuinely loved sharing their culture with these two strangers from thousands of miles away. Sure, the wedding was fake, but the warmth of our celebrants was as real as it gets, proving once again that the world truly is a very small place.

Papua New Guinea is not the kind of place you visit by yourself. Traveling through the country can be a hard, complicated slog, and you don't see a lot of tourist amenities. But with the help of the International Committee of the Red Cross, I was able to get to the heart of a country that still remains a mystery to much of the world. The committee's mission in this part of the globe is to mitigate the effects of tribal warfare, which is ongoing; to rebuild health clinics and provide water for schools; and to tend to the health and safety of the indigent. It was an honor to hang out with those folks. You don't hear very much about them on the nightly news, but their work in Papua New Guinea is important.

I've often been teased for saying "amazing!" a lot, and sometimes I overdo it. But over the course of seven days in Papua New Guinea, I was in a constant state of amazement. From the first moment I set eyes on these incredible people—and they looked back at me—it was an instant love story. In all my travels, that had never happened before.

At one point I asked a small group of Papua New Guineans to tell me what they loved. They were quick to answer.

"I love my strawberries!"

"I love my water!"

"I love my community!"

"I love my Papua New Guinea!"

And then this from a farmer, probably in his fifties: "I love you coming to my country. This is my solidarity. This is my soil."

When I look at the world map today, I no longer feel the pang of disappointment that I expressed to my dad all those years ago. Big deal if every little speck of an island already has a name attached to it—because I can assure you, what you'll find on them will most definitely leave you in awe of our beautiful and diverse world.

THE PLANET WARRIORS

When I was a little boy, I never understood why the Dead Sea was called the Dead Sea. For one thing, it's technically a lake; for another, how can a body of water be dead? I didn't even know it was sick.

The answer, I eventually learned, lies in the sea's crazy salt levels, which are so high that fish and other sea creatures cannot survive in it. Hence, the name. But that doesn't stop throngs of humans from flocking to it every year. Carved into the blond sands of the Negev Desert, on the borders of Israel, Palestine, and Jordan, the Dead Sea was a frequent holiday destination for my family when I was growing up. Some of my favorite childhood memories took place on its muddy banks.

But everything good must come to an end, and in this case, the end is deadly serious: the Dead Sea is dying. Industrial buildings are draining its water, inflow rivers are drying up, and the sea's once healthy hairline is receding at a rate of three feet per year. That's especially dangerous because, as the water pulls inward, the surface of the shoreline collapses, causing catastrophic sinkholes to suddenly appear—thousands of them, some as deep as eight stories. Now, my favorite sea is surrounded by warning signs that scream DANGER! SINKHOLES AHEAD.

Yet if you find yourself saddened by this dire health report from the Dead Sea, here's some encouraging news: for every ill that's inflicted on our planet—from pollution to littering to global warming—there's an equal and opposite effort to fix it. Yes, it's true, humans are killing the environment, but some humans are trying to make it better, too. I call these men and women Planet Warriors, and around the world, they are turning death sentences into rebirths. It took me a thousand days of travel to find these inspiring individuals, and having watched them at work, I am as optimistic as ever. As the legendary anthropologist Margaret Mead has been famously quoted, "Never doubt that a small group of thoughtful, committed citizens can change the world. Indeed, it's the only thing that ever has."

ZANZIBAR **SHE WANTS YOUR GLASS**

Floating thirty-one miles off the coast of Tanzania is the African island of Zanzibar, known worldwide for its heavenly spices and drop-dead beauty. And it's people like Lou Van Reemst who are fighting to preserve that splendor. Lou is an industrial design engineer who works with Bottle-up, a company that's on a mission to rid

the island of the tons of glass waste left by tourists on its beaches and streets. Lou is so passionate about her work that she will patiently watch you finish your bottle of beer just so she can personally take the empty from your hand. Once she does, she and her team will add it to the hundreds of other bottles they've collected and crush them into tiny bits, add cement, and mold them into functioning bricks that can be used to build houses in a more sustainable way. For every one house built from these bricks, Lou told me, she and Bottle-up protect the earth from fifty thousand littered bottles. These are Planet Warriors.

ECUADOR THEY BUILD HOUSES FROM MILK BOXES

In the balmy climes of Ecuador, a green-minded company called Ecuaplastic has perfected the same kind of creative recycling as Bottle-up, only with discarded juice and milk containers. Ecuaplastic is operated by an army of intrepid trash collectors who are expert in the art of stooping down and picking up. They gather an average of eleven million discarded milk cartons every month and then hand them off to a factory that cleans, shreds, and presses them into slabs of lightweight but sturdy chipboard that can be used in the manufacture of everything from furniture to roof tiling to place mats. I spent the day with these tireless Planet Warriors, and they took me to a house that was built entirely from 1.2 million milk boxes. That's a lot of dedication—and a lot of milk.

DENMARK **THE KAYAK KING**

It was along the legendary canals of Copenhagen that I met Tobias Weber-Andersen, an eco-entrepreneur who has figured out a clever way to ensure that those canals retain their romantic charm. Tobias is the devoted Planet Warrior behind GreenKayak, a homegrown company that rents out its sleek fleet of kayaks free of charge. But there's one condition to the rental: paddlers must collect the garbage from the water's surface and bring it back to the shore. I took one of these little cruises, and it was downright fun. You're issued a special trash-plucker (picture a long fishing rod with a trigger at one end and a retractable claw on the other), along with a bucket to store your garbage booty. Then you set sail and scoop up whatever you can find—coffee cups, bottle caps, candy wrappers, random stuff I couldn't even identify. By the time you've finished your one-hour spin through the canals, you've helped save the environment while saving $65 on the rental. According to Tobias's statistics, one single kayak can net three tons of trash in less than a year.

SRI LANKA **THE POOP TROOPER**

Planet Warrior Thusitha Ranasinghe, an entrepreneurial conservationist in the island nation of Sri Lanka, arguably has the crappiest job in the world—and that's a good thing. In 1997, Thusitha began growing concerned about the increasingly stormy relationship between Sri Lankans and the estimated six thousand elephants that roam the land—from deadly rampages to crop-trampling to poaching by the humans. Wouldn't it be great, he mused, if someone could bring together human and elephant in a peaceful and productive way? That's when he founded Eco-Maximus, an award-winning enterprise that uses elephant dung (aka, poop) to produce high-quality paper goods. The idea isn't as disgusting as it sounds. Turns out that because elephants are vegetarian, their massive mounds of  manure are filled with fiber, making it perfect for paper production. But the process is meticulous. After the elephant provides the, er, raw material, the poop goes through ten days of washing and boiling to remove the yuck factor, then it's dried, cleaned, dyed, compressed, smoothed, and cut into real paper products that are sold in more than thirty countries. And all of this comes from the dung of just eight elephants, because each one of them poops about sixteen times a day. Not only has Thusitha built himself a business, he's raising awareness about an endangered species, saving local forests, and providing jobs for underprivileged Sri Lankans who live in rural villages. Wow!

SEYCHELLES **CORAL COMMANDOS**

Floating peacefully in the Indian Ocean nine hundred miles off the East African coast are the Seychelles, the breathtaking archipelago nation that has captured hearts for centuries. Once you set foot on its visa-free, tropical shores, you'll understand why it's hugely popular as a honeymoon destination. Fringed in pale white sands and adrift in glassy blue waters, the Seychelles scream romance at every turn. But not all is so alluring beneath the waves. Because of a host of environmental ills—global warming, pollution, overfishing, aggressive snorkeling—the islands' fragile coral reefs are steadily dying; some scientists predict that by the end of the century, their rate of destruction will outpace their ability to restore themselves. That's why I was happy to fork over $35 to the coral adoption program run by the volunteer Planet Warriors of the Marine Conservation Society Seychelles. It works like this: You visit their kiosk on the beach, select a piece of live coral from a display case, pay your donation, and receive a certificate of adoption. Then a volunteer straps on diving gear, plunges into the ocean, and gently plants the fresh coral alongside its vanishing step-siblings. Unlike with a real adopted child, you won't get to watch your baby grow—but grow it will. And just like a real parent, you'll take pride in knowing that you've helped give life to a new generation.

THE GALÁPAGOS ISLANDS
NO BUTTS ABOUT HIM

It was during the week I spent in the environmental sanctuary of the Galápagos Islands, about six hundred miles off the coast of Ecuador, that I made the acquaintance of Miguicho Nicotina Asesina, a sixty-eight-year-old former fisherman who had lived a hard life of debt and alcohol before finally turning things around at age fifty-three, when he taught himself to read and write. Armed with his new power to learn about the world around him, Miguicho began a personal crusade to tidy up his own environment—simply by picking up cigarette butts he found on the streets. Before long, this mundane neighborhood cleanup campaign turned into a full-throttle mission, and by the time I met Miguicho, he'd already picked up about

seven hundred thousand butts. But he didn't stop there. Instead of just tossing the refuse into the nearest trash can, Miguicho used the butts to create colorful public sculptures to raise awareness about littering. Miguicho is a Planet Warrior, Picasso-style.

PERU HE SAVED A LAKE

Meet Marino Morikawa, a Peruvian-Japanese scientist who pretty much defines the passion and vision it takes to be a Planet Warrior. In 2010, Marino was heartbroken to learn that his favorite childhood lake in Peru's Cascajo wetlands had become contaminated, not unlike 40 percent of the world's lakes and rivers. But rather than give up hope, Marino took a sabbatical from his studies, secured a loan, depleted his savings, stepped into the lab, and created a 100 percent organic solution that successfully separates contaminated particles from healthy water. Satisfied with the performance of his potion, he whipped up a ton of the stuff; dumped it into the lake; treated the water with biofilters, nanotechnology, and crazy biology; and turned what had once been a dirty, algae-ridden swamp back into the crystalline blue lake of his youth. Gone were the parasites, bacteria, and pollution; and by the following year, birds had returned to the lake's shores, as did people. "Why doesn't everyone do this?" I asked Marino. "Because it's expensive and very hard," he told me. "But it's not impossible."

JOURNEY'S END

MALTA, DAY 1,000

I write this sentence with tears in my eyes.

Over the course of one thousand days, I made one thousand videos. I had promised that daily delivery in my very first video, nearly three years earlier, and I stood by that promise. Never missed a day—not even once.

"I don't know how I did it," I told my viewers in my final video on Day 1,000.

Now that I have reached the end of another journey—this book—I want to be more open than ever. And I think the best way to do this is by explaining how difficult that final video was to make.

It was 5:00 a.m. on January 5, 2019. I was in Malta. I'd chosen that particular country for Nas Daily's final video for several reasons. It's beautiful. Its people are welcoming and kind. And, most important, Malta holds a special place in my heart. My first trip there 276 days earlier had been one of my greatest memories of Nas Daily. The reception we were given by the people and the government of Malta was extraordinary, and for the first time, I felt like we'd really made a difference in a country.

And on a personal level, Malta made me feel special—like I was doing something worthwhile. Something that mattered.

But there in that hotel room on my final morning, I was exhausted. I had spent the majority of the night staring at my camera "with no words in my mouth" (as we say in Arabic), just endless thoughts. But how could I summarize those thousand days in just one minute? Perhaps a good way to begin was by looking back at the beginning of my life.

I grew up as a middle child, and according to studies on birth order, that's not always such a great spot to be in. The kid stuck in the middle doesn't always command the respect that's usually bestowed on the eldest child nor the adoration that is typically lavished on the youngest. So quite often middle children are left feeling ignored, as if their voices don't matter. And that, says the research, can damage their self-esteem.

I'd be lying if I didn't say that's the way it played out in my house. I never for a moment felt unloved by my parents—they're the best in the world—but I did feel lost in the shadow of my older brother, and I felt jealous of

my younger sister. My opinions didn't seem to carry much weight in the family, so after a while I stopped expecting attention, because it seemed like very few eyes were on me. More often than not, I was left alone with my quiet thoughts.

And my childhood wasn't the only issue. There was also my village. When I was growing up, Arraba's population was no more than twenty thousand, and the village mindset was simple: *You are born here and you die here.* There was no glass ceiling of success in Arraba—only a concrete one—and that applied to men and women alike. On top of all that, it was a Muslim village, which made me feel only more confined. Even today, it is significantly harder for a Muslim kid from a small village to command the same attention from the world as, say, a white kid from New York City.

So, yes, from my childhood to my village to my religion, it was tough for this kid to be heard. I felt like I was one out of billions.

That's not uncommon. As you read these words, innumerable humans around the planet don't have the same voice as the ones in power. This isn't just my opinion—this is a fact. The majority of the world's population is expected to follow, not lead. And from very early on, the child in me realized that he'd been born in a place where he was meant to fall in line, not step to the front of it.

But one day, I stumbled on a quotation from Steve Jobs that left a lasting impression on me. It put into words the very thoughts that had always nagged at me:

Life can be much broader once you discover one simple fact. And that is, everything around you that you call life was made up by people who were no smarter than you. And you can change it. You can influence it. You can build your own things that other people can use. Once you learn that, you'll never be the same again.

You'll never be the same again.

Wow. Those words were like an electric current that shot through my body. The mere notion that this middle child from a Muslim village in the Middle East could actually make a mark on the world changed everything.

And just like that, I was off to the races.

When I began Nas Daily on April 10, 2016, I made a commitment to learn as much about the world as I possibly could, and to document every moment of it.

I wanted to experience the culture in the Philippines, the natives of New Zealand, the nature of Iceland, the challenges of Israel, and the struggles of Palestine.

I wanted to capture the sunrise in Myanmar, the sunset in Chile, the magnificence of the Galápagos, and the compassion of Canada.

I wanted to lie on the beaches of the Seychelles and climb the cliffs of the Himalayas and wander the deserts of Morocco.

I wanted to explore the differences between men and women in the Maldives, speak the slang of Australia, marvel at the ecology of Singapore, and celebrate the generosity of Armenia.

Video by video, my personality began to emerge. I developed opinions and original thoughts. And I was aggressive. Very aggressive. I inserted myself into every video I made, not in an effort to become some self-anointed screen star, but rather to submerge myself in the waters of humanity—just the way I did, quite literally, in the waters of the Ganges River in Varanasi, India.

I put myself—and my thoughts—out there for the world to see, and to my complete surprise, people actually cared about my videos and my opinions. They watched me and they listened to me and they followed my journey. And they did this by the millions.

Nas Daily exploded. It became the talk of the town. The talk of villages. The talk of cities. It appeared on the news and across the internet. And many of those videos landed in ways that I least expected. They helped get people out of prison. They pulled viewers through depression. They put me in the company of presidents and prime ministers. In the United States alone, my videos reached seventy million people—*20 percent of the entire population.* By Day 1,000, they had amassed four billion views.

Nas Daily had turned into a global media channel—an astonishing achievement I never could have predicted. People began approaching me on the street and in restaurants and in airports. "Good job!" they'd say. "You inspire me!" "I love your videos!"

Yet as grateful as I was for the love and support, I had not embarked on this journey for compliments or for fame. I had no hidden agendas or ulterior motives. I just wanted to make videos and see whether I could somehow, in some way, have an impact on this world. Any impact. That's why I put so much effort into them—because I genuinely cared.

And when everyone cared back, I was humbled, and shocked, and deeply thankful.

So at 5:00 a.m. on January 5, 2019, as I wiped my eyes and took a few deep breaths before facing my camera and pressing the red button one last time, Steve Jobs's words once again ran through my mind.

The world is built by people no smarter than you.

This is why there are tears in my eyes as I write these sentences. Because this village kid finally built something bigger than himself.

Steve Jobs said something else that is also worth pondering: "You can poke life and push in and something will pop out the other side." And that, I think, was my greatest takeaway from Nas Daily. If more and more people from around this beautiful planet push in, something surely will pop out.

We can speak and be heard.

We can move mountains.

We can touch hearts.

We can change the world.

ACKNOWLEDGMENTS

Like Nas Daily itself, this book was an undertaking that required teamwork, passion, commitment, patience, friendship, love, and a whole lot of sleepless nights. To that end, I owe oceans of thanks to all those who helped me put it together.

Heartfelt appreciation to my Nas Daily family, who over the course of three years have become indispensable to our ongoing journey and irreplaceable as friends. Agon Hare, you are the most selfless person I have ever met. Thank you for your incredible patience, your amazing work ethic, and your crazy personality. Without your coolness, intelligence, and hard work, Nas Daily would not be the Nas Daily it is today. You rock, man. I can't wait to attend your concert.

Thank you, as well, to my agent, Brian DeFiore, who instantly saw the potential for Nas Daily to leap from the internet to bookshelves, and who worked his signature brand of magic to make that happen. I offer similar hugs to my intrepid team at HarperOne, for passionately pursuing, embracing, and delivering on this book—and especially to my editor, Sydney Rogers, whose creative vision and gentle wisdom are evident on every page.

Thank you to the new friends I met around the planet who fed the soul of Nas Daily at just the right moment in just the right way: To Ariel and Christine from Duma Works, bless you for inviting me to Kenya and forcing me to start this thing called Nas Daily. Tim Njiru, thanks for meeting me on Day 12 in Kenya and inspiring me to keep going. And Yusuf Omar, meeting you in India opened my eyes to just how big this could get. Thank you for that.

I am forever grateful for those unexpected encounters over the course of 1,000 days that taught me about the depth of the human heart. Nas in Bangalore, I will never forget the way you took me in when I was sick. Roi in the Philippines, thank you for buying me food when I was pretending I lost my wallet—you embody the true spirit of the Filipino. And Sabrina Iovino, thank you for taking a chance on me.

To Fidji Simo, Garrett Gottesman, and everyone else at Facebook, kudos for building out the best product in the world. And to Brandon Stanton of *Humans of New York*, you were my first source of inspiration, and I'm honored to call you a friend. Your work will live for years, and you are the main reason this book exists.

Endless thanks to Janine Sapinoso and Ruth Castillo, for their dogged transcription of more than a quarter-million words of Nas Daily scripts, and their loyalty and enthusiasm for the project throughout; and to Daniel Loftus and Bridgette Kluger, for pinch-hitting on transcriptions when Janine and Ruth were giving their aching hands a rest.

Thanks also to the three Davids—David Rensin, for his savvy counsel on how to surf the turbulent waters of book publishing (while having fun doing it!); David Tabatsky, for his unerring eye and ear in the art of bringing videos and drone footage to the printed page; and David Slavin, for his good humor and guidance—and for gamely watching more Nas Daily videos than he bargained for.

A big across-the-pond high five to Jan Pfeil, for his early read of the manuscript and for his unique (and highly amusing) perspective on our wacky world. And loads of gratitude to Jonathan Levine, Marlo Thomas, and Alene Hokenstad, each of whom rode shotgun on this crazy ride, offering invaluable and unwavering support every step of the way.

Salamat and *grazzi* to the nations of the Philippines and Malta—and their people—for their warmth and hospitality, and for helping to put Nas Daily, quite literally, on the map. And thank you to the nation of Singapore for showing me—and the rest of the world—what an amazing country should look like.

To Alyne, my wonderful girlfriend, you have the patience of an elephant, the joy of a dolphin, and the fire of a fox. Thank you for finding the heart of Nas Daily and for helping me to grow, both professionally and spiritually.

And love and more love to Mom, Dad, Brother, Sister, and Younger Brother (Omaima, Ziad, Tarek, Naya, and Mohammed Yassin) for giving me the freedom to pursue my dreams. Without your constant support, I wouldn't be here. You watched every single video even before anyone else did, and for that—and so much more—I am indebted to you.

And most of all, thank you to you, the reader. Without you, I am nothing.

ABOUT THE AUTHOR

Nuseir "Nas" Yassin is a Palestinian-Israeli who grew up in the village of Arraba in the country's northern district. Fluent in Arabic, Hebrew, and English, he left Israel in 2010 to attend Harvard University on a full scholarship, where he graduated in 2014 with degrees in economics and computer science. Twenty months into his first post-college job as a software coder for Venmo, Nas made the decision that would change his life: to quit his job, gather his savings, and travel the world, sharing his adventures and discoveries on his dedicated Facebook page, Nas Daily. On January 5, 2019, Nas reached Day 1,000 of Nas Daily, having garnered an international audience of 12 million followers and 4.5 billion video impressions. He continues to post weekly videos on Nas Daily and has relocated to Singapore, where he is launching a media and video company with his best friends.